Reclaim

DR AHONA GUHA is a clinical and forensic psychologist, and a survivor with lived experience of complex trauma. *Reclaim: understanding complex trauma and those who abuse* is her first book. She works with victims of abuse and trauma, and clients with a range of other difficulties — such as anxiety, depression, perfectionism, burnout, and relationship problems. She also works with perpetrators of harmful behaviours to assess risk, and provides treatment to reduce the risk they pose to others. She writes widely for the media on matters related to mental health, health, social justice, and equity. Her work has appeared in *The Age*, *The Guardian*, *The Saturday Paper*, and in *Breathe Magazine*, and on SBS and the ABC. She has a strong focus on social justice and seeks a world free of violence and harm, directing her work towards remedying the psychological drivers of these behaviours. She is passionate about equity, diversity, and advocacy and capacity-building for those historically marginalised.

Reclaim

understanding complex trauma
and those who abuse

Dr Ahona Guha

SCRIBE
Melbourne • London

Scribe Publications
2 John St, Clerkenwell, London, WC1N 2ES, United Kingdom
18–20 Edward St, Brunswick, Victoria 3056, Australia
3754 Pleasant Ave, Suite 100, Minneapolis, Minnesota 55409, USA

Published by Scribe 2023

Typeset in Adobe Caslon by the publishers

Printed and bound in the UK by CPI Group (UK) Ltd, Croydon CR0 4YY

Scribe is committed to the sustainable use of natural resources and the use of paper
products made responsibly from those resources.

978 1 914484 62 9 (UK edition)
978 1 922585 68 4 (Australian edition)
978 1 957363 41 7 (US edition)
978 1 761385 09 4 (ebook)

Catalogue records for this book are available from the National Library of Australia
and the British Library.

scribepublications.co.uk
scribepublications.com.au
scribepublications.com

For Kim — for walking with me.

&

For my clients — you inspire me daily with the trust you place in me, your willingness to change, and your courage in the face of darkness and pain. Thank you for allowing me the honour of walking alongside you.

Contents

A Note

There are a few things to note before you start reading this book.

This is a book about complex trauma and abuse. It discusses a range of troubling issues, and mentions child abuse, sexual violence, intimate partner violence, coercive control, stalking, and physical abuse. I have not sanitised this material for comfort — it is important to clearly demonstrate the nature of the difficulties that people experience and live with — but nor have I presented gratuitous detail that might overwhelm you. As you read, I encourage you to be aware of your own emotional responses to the material and any trauma history you might carry — and to give yourself permission to pause reading if any distressing emotional experience occurs.

I have focused on trauma and abuse through an objective lens, to best help everyone understand these harms. Sometimes objectivity can feel like invalidation in the face of deeply felt emotion and painful experiences. My statements are designed to inform and to acknowledge the complex nuances of these areas; they are not intended to invalidate or dismiss distress. This book is not intended to be a replacement for professional advice, nor is it designed to be used as a resource by those currently in crisis.

The principle of confidentiality is paramount in therapy — clients expect and deserve that their stories will be held in utmost confidence, and that any breaches of these boundaries will occur only in certain circumstances, and with full awareness of the ethical implications. Confidentiality is an especially strong guiding principle when working with traumatised clients who have had their boundaries repeatedly breached. In this book, I have balanced the need to provide some clinical material to convey the richness and depth of trauma work with maintaining the confidentiality of my clients. After careful consideration, I have decided that composite cases[1] are the most ethical means of illustrating my points. In each case, I have utilised the general clinical dynamics and issues that come up when working with trauma clients while making sure that specific details (such as names and ages) are fictional. Many clients with abuse histories have similar troubles, and I have been able to create realistic and accurate composites by building case studies around the symptom clusters I commonly see in my practice.

The clients I have described from my work in forensic psychology have also undergone a similar process. Adrian (Chapter 6) is an amalgam of many of the stalkers and intimate partner violence offenders I have seen. People who engage in offences of this type often share some characteristics, behaviours, and histories, and I have used my knowledge of the risk literature and the hundreds of police reports I have read to create his character. Madison (Chapter 2) and Kate (Chapter 5) are also composite cases, based on my work with female clients in the forensic system. I have written of some horrific trauma histories within the correctional system, and some readers might think that these histories are immediately identifying. Unfortunately, these histories are common, though often unspoken. Most of my female forensic clients were severely sexually and physically abused by caregivers, and their history is not enough to identify them — nonetheless, I've changed key circumstances to mitigate this slight risk and have only provided details when necessary to illustrate a clinical point.

Finally, I need to say that while I work for a public forensic mental health service, all views expressed in this book are my own only and are not representative of the views held within my organisation, or of the broader legal, correctional, and mental health systems within which I work. Any discussion of specific mental health or correctional settings utilises information that is available in the public domain. I discuss a range of personal experiences in this book and acknowledge that my recollection of events is imperfect and that other people's memories may differ. When I have discussed real events, names and identifying characteristics have been removed.

The tasks of a psychologist and a writer often diverge, though I consider that truth-telling and advocacy for those whose voices have been ignored are the tasks of both. In the Sisyphean task of merging these two roles, I have been guided above all by my own ethics and values, and desire to effect change — while openly and compassionately acknowledging realistic systemic limitations.

Introduction

The early years of the 2020s were exceedingly hard for many of us. We lived through a pandemic and all its attendant difficulties, including separations from those closest to us, illness and death, despair, collapsed health systems, and massive declines in mental health. Though my work remained stable, there were times I found myself shaken by a deep existential terror. Nothing felt meaningful, I felt utterly disconnected from everyone I loved, and I had no hope for humanity, or myself.

These terrifying dark thoughts and feelings made sense when placed in the context of a global pandemic. The COVID-19 pandemic brought to the world a type of collective trauma on a scale previously unknown in our lifetimes. This came not only in the form of health and economic forces, but also relational and social ones: many of us were ripped apart from each other, left bereft of hope, and struggled through without the capacity to band together. When given the opportunity to connect, some of us declined, exhausted and terrified of re-entry to the world. Our reactions have mirrored those of survivors of serious childhood neglect,[1] who often demonstrate complete withdrawal and an inability to connect with other people.

Beyond the reach of the pandemic, those years brought other traumas front and centre in Australia. A survivor of child sexual abuse, Grace Tame, was awarded Australian of the Year for her excellent work on advocacy for victims. The coroner's report on an Aboriginal woman's death in custody noted that her death was wholly preventable and related to systemic and individual failures. The Nadesalingam

5

refugee family from Biloela continued to quietly suffer medical neglect, separation from community, and the after-effects of the experiences that led to them fleeing Sri Lanka. Numerous refugees were imprisoned for years in tiny, airless hotel rooms in Melbourne.

Globally, race-driven violence continued, and tensions catalysed into action and riots after George Floyd's death. Women were killed by current and former partners. Military troops withdrew from Afghanistan, creating scenes of chaos and turmoil, and dread of the years to come as people in Afghanistan, especially women, experienced a return to life under the Taliban regime. Russia invaded Ukraine. Roe v. Wade was overturned, leaving millions of American women without safe and legal access to abortions.

This is not an exhaustive list, of course, but just the ones that immediately spring to my mind. Many people remain in a state of interpersonal flux and withdrawal, as they attempt to make sense of that which has occurred, and struggle to create some internal stability.

Our worlds may seem fractured, with no sense of certainty, no control, and feelings of impending danger and doom.

This is the world a complex trauma survivor lives in daily.

I am a clinical and forensic psychologist in Melbourne, Australia. Clinical psychologists work with people who have serious mental health difficulties, while forensic psychologists work in those in-between spaces where legal systems intersect with mental health systems. The interests I developed during my training mean that the bulk of my work takes place in forensic mental health, with those who have harmed other people in some serious way and have concurrent mental health needs. My doctoral research[2] explored the long-term mental and physical health impacts of childhood sexual abuse and found that people with histories of child sex abuse were significantly more likely to seek higher levels of medical and mental health care for a wide range of reasons and were also at higher risk of premature death than members of the general population. Trauma inflicts mental damage, but its effects extend into the domain of physical health, too. Rates of suicide in trauma survivors are high;[3] sometimes a history of abuse can feel so difficult to carry that death appears preferable.

The emotional and behavioural difficulties caused by early and complex relational traumas (i.e., traumas that happen within relationships) are immense, and flow through from the individual to entire social structures. They often bring with them flurries of psychological and life chaos for the individuals, and for all the professionals and systems involved in supporting them. Trauma-related difficulties compound other existing psychological disorders, complicating the process of recovery. Many individuals with serious psychiatric issues and a large proportion of people incarcerated in prison have complex trauma histories. While trauma does not cause all psychiatric difficulties and does not make people engage in crime, it often kickstarts a hard journey.

There is still much disagreement about what constitutes a traumatic event. While the DSM-V and ICD-11 (the main psychiatric diagnostic manuals) provide some guidance as to the definitions of trauma, these definitions are still largely left open to interpretation. The DSM-V defines trauma as 'actual or threatened death, serious injury, or sexual violence', while the ICD-11 defines complex trauma as 'exposure to an event or series of events of an extremely threatening or horrific nature, most commonly prolonged or repetitive events from which escape is difficult or impossible'.

The term 'complex' refers to the cumulative and multiple nature of the trauma, as well as to its wide-ranging impacts, and not to the survivor themselves. I use the terms complex and relational trauma interchangeably in this book. When I say 'relationship', I refer to all types of relationships, whether intimate, platonic, familial, or casual. Every micro-connection we form with another human being is a relationship, and a potential conduit to healing or harm.

Survivors and therapists in the field often use a broader definition than that proposed by the DSM-V and the ICD-11. Terms such as 'threatening' and 'horrific' remain open to interpretation. Overall, I consider that any event that involves physical, sexual, or psychological harm being inflicted upon one person by another may be considered traumatic in nature, whether a single event or a series of cumulative and compounding events. People have different responses to traumatic events, and what feels devastating for one person may not have the same impact on another. Protective factors (such as the presence of safe attachment figures) and early intervention can also reduce the impacts of abuse. While the body experiences and holds trauma, trauma also causes fractures in the ways we think, feel, and hold memories. The body and the brain can both hold these memories; trauma won't be embodied for every survivor. Also, not every survivor will struggle over their lifespan; for many people, safe lifestyles, good relationships, work, and educational engagement go a long way towards mitigating its effects.

Relational traumas are peculiar to the human condition. No other species deliberately inflicts harm on another of its kind, except in the pursuit of food or procreation. Our prefrontal cortices have given us a wide and wonderful array of complex cognitive processes, and while these processes have allowed us to build complex lives with incredible social depth and richness, they have also at times allowed us to become aggressive or inflict pain on each other. We are complex social beings and while we may hurt each other, we also need each other. We live in a web of relationships, and we acquire many of our fundamental emotional skills through attachment with our primary caregivers. Relational traumas carry with them a specific sting: we rely on our social connections to mirror our existence in the world, and we can experience damage caused by other people as an assault on our core selves and identities. In addition, those we rely on for survival are often those who abuse, such as when a parent hurts a child.

When we speak about trauma, I have found both that the dialogue is centred around a limited range of symptoms and that certain survivors are seen as more 'palatable' than others. The public discourse often focuses on those who manifest their traumas in a range of socially acceptable ways — perhaps through low mood, anxieties, burnout, perfectionism, people-pleasing, insomnia, and overwork. While some people with complex trauma histories may indeed display these symptoms, many have much darker difficulties, including substance abuse and addiction, problems with managing emotion, self-harm and suicidality, eating disorders, difficulties with anger and aggression, impulsivity, and lifestyle chaos. Many survivors move through cycles of disorganisation and harm and often find themselves caught in punitive systems, including child protection systems, public mental health systems, and the correctional and carceral systems.

People who experience severe and protracted hurt within close relationships, such as parents or partners, often experience difficulties with their emotions, moods, approaches to the world, and lifestyles — leaving professionals flummoxed as their clients lurch from one crisis to the next. This remains especially true for those who react to their trauma in ways that are considered socially unacceptable or especially complex: by developing serious mental illnesses, by perpetrating violence or harm against other people, by becoming 'treatment resistant', 'difficult', 'hostile', 'dependent' or 'non-compliant'.

When we think about complex trauma it is essential to hold *all* survivors in mind — not just those we judge to be worthy of healing (typically those we see as being most like *us*). As a society and as individuals, we often focus on those we consider most worthy of healing, or those who have some form of potential. Facing the true aftermath of the most complex traumas and the systemic changes needed to address them can be overpowering, and many of us resort to blaming some victims for their behaviours, and trying to punish them, whether by withholding adequate psychological care, or by incarcerating instead of treating. In this book, I focus on all forms of complex trauma and do not shy away from talking about the darker post-traumatic behaviours I have witnessed.

I also find that we struggle to fully understand and adequately respond to the impacts of relational trauma, and the psychological factors underlying them. Many victims bounce from service to service, receiving piecemeal treatment for their various symptoms, and gaining limited understanding of the broad psychological patterns that underlie their pain. Some of these victims are retraumatised by the type of care they receive; some frequently enter institutional models of care (such as hospitals and prisons) due to a complex mix of difficulties originating from trauma responses.

I currently work for a public forensic mental service, assessing and treating those who present with a range of high-risk problem behaviours, including:[4] stalking, arson, sex offending, general violence, family violence, threats, and vexatious behaviours (such as using court systems and online forums to harass individuals). I also have a small number of private practice clients. In my private practice, I predominantly work with clients who have experienced complex trauma and abuse.

My forensic work involves working with clients who perpetrate aggression and relational traumas on other people; individuals who have killed other people; mothers who have hurt or killed their children; people who have stalked, raped, set fires, threatened, and assaulted other people. All my forensic clients have hurt other people. Most of them have also been victims. I use the words victim and survivor interchangeably through this book, in a context-dependent manner. I am aware of the debates in this field around terminology but have chosen to use these words separately, because — to put it bluntly — some victims are not given the opportunity to become survivors. When I say victim, I don't mean to disrespect or disempower someone who has experienced abuse; I am homing in on the unwilling, painful experience of being harmed and victimised by another individual.

Those who abuse or hurt other people are often misunderstood; their actions are not often considered when attempting to understand trauma. The public conversation has adopted a few neat explanations for harm, including recourse to concepts such as narcissism and psychopathy or to broad sociological explanations such as 'men's choice to inflict violence against women'. Frequently, people who harm other people are reviled and seen as monsters. We give simplistic reasons for harmful behaviour because we find neat categories easier to understand and manage. It is easier to place people within either the 'victim' or 'perpetrator' category, or to believe that there is something innate within a perpetrator that sets them apart from us and makes them capable of inflicting hurt on other people. If we can hold these dichotomies in mind, then we can safely hate those who harm and can separate ourselves from them, remaining resolute in the knowledge of our essential goodness. However, these beliefs belie the truth: harmful behaviour arises from a confluence of factors,[5] and many of us, in certain circumstances, would behave in problematic ways.[6]

The true explanations for abusive behaviour lie deeper than we think, sometimes in personal trauma, personality, and psychological functioning, sometimes in systems that protect, support, and collude — but most often, in combination.

There are few monsters in this life, but there are many damaged people who damage other people.

It is difficult to walk the tightrope of working with both trauma victims and those who inflict harm. I see these roles as complementary, not opposed. When I work with people who abuse, I am always struck by how many of them were hurt themselves before they started behaving in ways that remain unfathomable to most of us.

A history of trauma does not cause violence; violence and harm have multiple causes and most people with these histories never hurt other people. However, trauma can act as a predisposing factor in some cases (usually in conjunction with a range of other factors, such as substance use), and it is rare to see someone who has inflicted serious harm and has not had some form of early childhood adversity themselves. This does not excuse their behaviour or mean that we don't protect ourselves from them, it just means that we can explain and understand their behaviour in the context of what they suffered.

When working with victims and abusers, I hold in mind my essential values-based professional remit — keeping people safe and making the world a slightly better place. While I can't help everyone or control everything, understanding and working compassionately with those who harm allows me to contribute to reducing the hurt and harm being inflicted. I also find it helpful to use my knowledge of perpetration to support victims with identifying, understanding, and protecting themselves from those who might abuse. There are many myths about trauma and the nature of perpetrators, and to fully understand and protect against harm within relationships, we must understand the people perpetrating it. We cannot manage that to which we remain ignorant.

In many ways, my trauma clients provide me with a bulwark of courage, hope, and healing when I'm faced with the difficulties of working in the forensic space. In them, I see a desire to heal, and the capacity to approach sustained change despite injuries inflicted — and this encourages and strengthens me when my courage flags.

This book is designed to be a guide to evidence-based psychological frameworks that can aid in understanding the nature of complex traumas, the tasks of recovery, the nature of those who perpetrate abuse, and broader issues involved in service provision and trauma management. It contains a blend of research and the experiential and clinical, and is drawn from my training and experience in clinical and forensic psychology, as well as my pre-psychology experiences in various social service roles, including as a residential care worker for children in state care, and a family violence support worker. It focuses on how people think and feel, what they believe, and relational/interpersonal structures that contribute to or protect against harm. While specific neurobiological and physiological processes underpin the effects of complex trauma, this book only delves into the psychological processes, with very brief summaries of neurobiological and physiological processes where appropriate. Several stalwarts[7] have already most excellently explored the neurobiology and physiology of trauma, and I refer you to their work if this aspect is of interest.

I want to make a specific note on gender here, too. Many books about trauma and abuse refer to victims almost exclusively as women and perpetrators as men. I don't subscribe to this dichotomy, as behaviour and difficulties are rarely so clearly gendered. I have worked with male and female victims and perpetrators of each type of harmful behaviour — including family violence, sexual violence, and general violence. Gender is a relevant factor for certain types of behaviours (such as sexual violence), and I discuss this as and when appropriate. However, I have also made attempts to use gender-neutral language as much as possible, and I consider it important to recognise that both genders experience and perpetrate harm, often with similar psychological factors underpinning these behaviours. Equally, certain behaviours have strong societal underpinnings, and it would be remiss not to talk about the impacts of sexualisation, power, and misogyny in relation to women's experiences of abuse. These discussions are nuanced and complex, and I have deliberately focused on research evidence, steering away from ideology but towards safety and respect for all.

I have my own history of experiencing and recovering from several traumas. This is not a book about my experiences, but I have shared this because I think it is vital to shift the narrative that survivors are broken and incapable of healing, and that trauma only happens to certain types of people. Historically, there has been great stigma attached to speaking about mental ill-health, and professionals are often discouraged from speaking about their own mental health difficulties, though pleasingly, I have seen a shift in this post-pandemic.

I will never stigmatise mental ill-health, and one of the most powerful ways I can ensure this is by owning my own journey. I will not speak about my traumas publicly — my story is my own, and I choose privacy — but I will share that I struggled for many years with difficulties caused by them. I now consider that I have recovered very well, but this process took much effort, financial investment in my mental health, time, and patience. I was failed by many people, and in many ways, before I found the right help. I had the privilege of being able to invest the time and resources needed into healing and I had a great desire to do so, to ensure I did not allow these difficulties to ravage my life or influence my work with my own clients. I was also lucky enough to find a psychologist who accompanied me on this journey, and who continues to hold a safe space for me. Not every survivor can find this or has the privilege of being able to focus so closely on their mental health.

This book is born from my training, my research into child sexual abuse, my work as a therapist at the coalface of trauma therapy and forensic mental health, and my own long-term therapy as a client. Many of us carry relational wounds. None of those wounds preclude us from being whole people. I hope this book can cast a light on some dark corners and hold a steady beam as we explore the various facets of relational trauma, the perpetration of abuse, and ways to climb above and beyond that which we might have suffered or seen inflicted.

I hope that above all, this book can bring hope.

1

Understanding Relational Trauma

Trauma is part of the cultural zeitgeist like never before.

I cannot look at social media without another infographic popping up, telling me about the ways it affects my relationships, my sleep, my work, and my body. Many of these infographics are reductive and exaggerated, but their very existence speaks to the way trauma and abuse have entered our cultural narrative. Numerous books on the subject have appeared on bookshelves, and several high-profile people have spoken publicly and courageously about their histories.

Trauma is a relatively well-known phenomenon but despite the ubiquity of the construct, it remains shrouded in confusion.

What exactly is a trauma?

What separates a trauma from a distressing, but not traumatic, event?

Why do some people heal after trauma, while others suffer?

What does a high-functioning survivor look like?

What does high functioning even mean?

Why does our conversation focus so closely on the more acceptable manifestations of trauma (perfectionism, anxiety, insomnia) and so little on the darker aspects (suicide, self-harm, drug use, offending)?

Why do so many survivors of relational trauma experience repeated victimisation? And why do systems that are ostensibly set up to help survivors so often retraumatise them?

Why do so many people with trauma histories struggle to find help?

Why do so many therapists struggle to appropriately recognise and treat trauma?

How do professionals cope when working with those with trauma histories?

What is vicarious trauma?

These are all relevant — and difficult — questions.

As a trauma-trained psychologist, I straddle an uncomfortable divide. I am familiar with many manifestations of trauma, and I work hard to help clients accept and manage their histories without minimising or ignoring their pain. I also work just as hard to help them build a realistic sense of themselves as people *outside*, and *above*, their experiences. I ask clients to hold their distress and accept it, while reminding them that they don't need to label distress as 'trauma' to legitimise it. However, I also encourage clients to label their difficult experiences as trauma when this naming appears helpful.

I appreciate conversations about trauma within popular culture and the normalisation of discussions about mental health, but flinch when I see the colloquialisation of trauma and abuse or find that these concepts have been usurped by people without mental health training for financial gain. The expansion of the construct of 'trauma' is ultimately, I believe, a positive step, but there is still a distinction to be made between traumatic experiences, and those that may feel difficult, but remain within the bounds of normal human functioning.

Over the past few decades, there has been a significant change in how we see trauma. We've started to recognise that events outside the limits of the physically harmful may also be traumatic in their impacts on the psyche. This gives people a frame with which to recognise the nature of their experiences and to understand the distress that certain events might have caused them. Being able to name and label events helps our brain make sense of them, allowing us to manage the distress with greater ease.

Despite these positives, there are also some difficulties inherent in the way we speak about trauma — often with blithe ignorance of the stark realities of the fractures it can create in the psyche. Trauma is often colloquialised on social media, such that the term is commonly and incorrectly used to explain many common psychological patterns (burnout, always being busy, not sleeping well, compulsive scrolling on social media, and people-pleasing are examples), and a range of relatively normal and adaptive (i.e., something that helps people cope well in their environment) behaviours.

Trauma bonding, fawning, polyvagal activation, attachment difficulties, narcissism, co-dependency, enmeshment — these are all phrases you might have come across, and many of them are derived from trauma literature. I don't mean to sound too doom and gloom, as there are also some excellent realistic representations of trauma in contemporary culture: the movie *Precious*, the Netflix series *Maid*,

Aimee's slowly creeping response to the sexual assault she experienced in Season 3 of the hit TV show *Sex Education*, the Man Booker Prize–winning tome *Shuggie Bain*. All of these contain realistic depictions of traumatic events and their psychological aftermath, without being sensationalist.

And yet, 'trauma' is bandied around as the reason for many ills, and it's not uncommon to see certain difficult or harmful behaviours quickly explained away as a manifestation of it. While there *is* broad truth underlying this phenomenon — trauma is complex, causes numerous psychological harms, and can underpin many difficulties — the phenomenon is far more complex and nuanced than the media has captured.

I suspect that people are talking more about trauma for several reasons.

First, decades of research experience and real-world living have built a strong body of knowledge attesting to the sweeping impacts of trauma on people's functioning and lives. Technological advances have allowed us to examine the brains of traumatised individuals, revealing the stark structural changes that happen when adversities occur at key developmental periods. We now know that veterans can continue to suffer from post-traumatic symptoms for decades after war, and that complete cures are not always possible. I caveat this by noting that there are several excellent therapies available now, and that many people will achieve symptom-free status with treatment. However, our initial optimism has worn off, as we see that the road to recovery is often rocky, with traumas, especially those that are complex and cumulative, being transmitted over generations. We have well-articulated systems of understanding post-traumatic responses, and we know that the effects of trauma cause broader ripples than intrusions (such as flashbacks or nightmares) alone.

It is not just shell-shock, it is life-shock.

Years of research and clinical experience have shown that

trauma is a key predisposing (i.e., something that may increase our vulnerability to developing mental health difficulties) factor that can underpin many emotional difficulties. It is much better understood now than in the past, largely thanks to the work of champions in the field, such as Bruce Perry, Judith Hermann, Alice Miller, and Bessel Van der Kolk. We know that its impacts are vast, and that a history of early relational trauma is an established risk factor for most psychiatric conditions, including those previously considered to be purely organic in nature, such as psychosis. Current writing on trauma is easy to access and absorb, far removed from the complex clinical esoterica of past decades. Mental health has become part of our lexicon in a manner it has never been before — and with this comes a concomitant increase in awareness of trauma as a primary insult that can shatter mental health.

We *know* more, so we *see* more.

Second, we are now able to focus less on the tasks of basic survival and have more cognitive resources available to ponder the bigger questions, as well as the capacity to engage in a shared discourse. In certain pockets, there is a greater thrust towards equity and parity and more people are starting to challenge the status quo. This often involves an examination of the harms that have been done to people and a recognition of trauma. People from diverse backgrounds have started to speak publicly about their lives and difficult histories, helping to normalise the conversation and paving ground for others to follow. Minorities have gained an expanded platform as we focus on representation, which has also cleared the way for finally understanding and addressing the systemic harms and aggressions inflicted on entire groups of people. However, each step towards greater equality brings a strong backlash, and it is common for powerful people to band together and strongly push against change. There are good examples of this in the way certain sections of the (rich, white, male) media treat survivors like Grace Tame.

Third, the reach of technology and social media has facilitated access to easy and overly simplistic information about complex mental health phenomena, often put forward by people who have limited or no formal qualifications in health or mental health. The concept creep around trauma is partly driven by people who want to harness the interest in trauma and abuse for their own benefit. Mental health terminology can be easily usurped for financial gain or social influence, which has resulted in several terms becoming part of our broader vocabulary (e.g., narcissism, attachment, gaslighting, manipulation, psychopathy) without most people having a true understanding of what they mean and how they might manifest. While writing this chapter, I saw a post on LinkedIn by a research institute in couples therapy, advising people of the signs of post-traumatic stress disorder (PTSD) after an affair. PTSD is a diagnosable mental health condition and requires involvment in, or witnessing of, a life-threatening incident. While an affair is immensely painful and confronting, it does not satisfy the basic diagnostic criterion for PTSD. However, people who experienced significant hurt after an affair (i.e., practically everyone who has had a partner who has engaged in infidelity) will relate to this notion, may believe that they have PTSD, and may be drawn into a range of courses and therapies proffered to 'heal' this PTSD.

When we lack deep knowledge of a subject, the human tendency is to seek cognitive shortcuts, also known as heuristics, and default to neat explanations for complex phenomena (e.g., anyone who is callous is a psychopath). Social media has trained our attention such that we have become like toddlers — entranced by bright colours, eye-catching dances, and catchy tunes, instead of being able to tolerate the slower and altogether harder graft of truly understanding complex phenomena. Trauma will never be adequately captured by a TikTok video or an Instagram reel.

Culturally, trauma has been presented as an explanation for numerous psychological and relational difficulties, and this has been adopted by many people without question. Western societies allow quick medicalisation and pathologising of experiences; this tendency has likely increased our willingness to identify trauma in normal experiences that may bring difficult feelings. We dislike aversive emotion and by naming something as trauma, perhaps we can access treatment for it and remove it from our lives — a far quicker and more palatable experience than simply noting that bad feelings and distress are part of our emotional lives and must sometimes be tolerated.

Social media also allows easy access to groupthink, such that people unconsciously fall into emulating the behaviours and thoughts of masses of other people, without being able to critically evaluate the information being provided. There *is* truth inherent in these cultural depictions of the impacts of trauma, but the mechanisms underpinning those impacts are often far more complex than presented.

In addition, I suspect that we struggle with relationships more than ever in our hyper-connected but extremely busy worlds. While I have little to back this up beyond my own clinical and personal experiences, it seems like structures of close relating — kindness, compassion, careful thought, and regard for other people — have drifted away in the currents of work, achievement, travel, side hustles, social media, online dating, and the relentless availability of an array of options. We treat other people like they are disposable, but we are also lonely, worry about our relationships, and struggle to grow connections. As we focus more on learning about relationships as a mechanism for trying to build better ones, we have started to think more carefully about the harms that have been, and can be, inflicted in relationships — and have developed a greater vocabulary around relational trauma.

Finally, when we talk about trauma, sometimes we are instead talking about its far-reaching *effects*, the long ripples into personality formation, lifestyle factors, health behaviours, and relationship difficulties. We are relational beings and trauma fundamentally fractures our capacity to relate, both to ourselves and to each other. We need a shorthand for talking about the impacts of trauma on people's selves, personalities, psychopathologies and defences, and so we use the word *trauma* itself, as some form of monolithic, static entity.

My main concern with the misuse of the word trauma is not that people use it too easily, but that we use it unthinkingly without full recognition of the many impacts of trauma. Without this recognition and accurate understanding of both the impacts, and the treatments available, survivors like Suzie will continue to struggle.

The first time I saw Suzie, she sat clenched at the edge of her chair, as if poised for flight. She looked brittle and fine-boned; everything about her was neat and *sharp*. Her collarbones pushed through her skin in deep grooves, and her linen shift was ironed into razor creases. A very slight tremor in her hands belied this seeming calm.

She looked like she didn't want to be there, as if some impulse had prodded her along against her will, marionetting her into my room.

'I'm just always so anxious,' she said. 'It's the worst when I have to present at board meetings, I always feel so stupid and can't find the words and just freeze up. Everyone else is so much better at work than me.'

Over the course of a year of therapy, we spoke about Suzie's history and tried to understand the roots of her difficulties with anxiety. I quickly established that she was a very high achiever, and was, indeed, not 'stupid' as she believed. She held a difficult role in the finance industry and managed a large team of professionals. On the outside, her life looked great — a great job, a stable relationship, travel, and friends.

On the inside, she remained beset by worry about being found wanting or being a 'fraud'. She experienced intense anxiety at work each day and overcompensated for her worries, taking on challenging tasks, refusing to rest, and remaining hypervigilant for any signs of disapproval. Her relationship was barely functional, and she co-existed with her partner, rarely coming together, or creating space for affection or intimacy. She wanted more closeness, but did not want to risk rejection.

'When I was sad the other day and said I wanted a hug and to talk, he asked me if it could wait until after he finished work.'

'What did you say?' I asked.

'Nothing. I started shaking after he left. I really wanted to purge.'

Even in her despair and sadness, she did not want to be seen as difficult, or to allow herself the vulnerability of anger. Instead, she resorted to coping mechanisms she had developed as an adolescent to soothe herself, including binging food and then purging (vomiting).

The theme of difficulties with relationships often arose in our work together, as we carefully tried to unpick the threads of Suzie's narrative and understand the reasons she made some of the choices she did. Over time, we recognised the incredibly difficult childhood she had faced, with parents who used substances, and a history of intense emotional neglect and sexual abuse, which was compounded by abusive relationships in early adulthood.

Suzie threw herself into work and achievement as a way of escaping from her unhappy childhood, and she believed that achievement and financial security meant she would never again be subject to the harms that she'd experienced from other people, effectively trying to compensate for the insecurity of her early years. She had very high standards for herself and a deep sense of inadequacy, created in the aftermath of many years of emotional abuse (she often talked about how her mother screamed at her, 'You can't do anything right, you should just die', and the way in which these words echoed in her mind whenever she thought she had failed). These traits manifested themselves in a range of ways, including difficulties with allowing people to be close to her in intimate or platonic relationships, tight control over her body size, disordered eating patterns, stress caused by lack of rest, and a deep belief that she was an imposter and would be 'caught' one day.

Once we worked on understanding the map of her traumas and responses, and allowed her to speak openly and fully about the harms done to her, some of Suzie's symptoms eased. She was still anxious at work, but this was much more manageable than it had been, and we knew that the work that we needed to do together had far deeper roots than simple work-related anxiety. This was very difficult for her to accept, but she reported experiencing a sense of freedom when she realised that some of the feelings she wrestled with were a by-product of what she had already faced rather than a sign that she was 'defective', 'too weak to cope', or 'just can't do relationships'. She understood, instead, that she believed deeply that she was defective and was not allowed to have physical or emotional needs; that her choice of partners and friends often reflected her beliefs that she did not deserve any care; and that she overcompensated for her belief that she was defective through intense achievement, never allowing herself to stop until she crashed.

What is complex or relational trauma?

Relational abuses are harms that occur within our relationships with other people. Most abuse can lead to trauma, though the term 'trauma' itself is used to denote the *impacts* of abuse and harm. Not every act of abuse leads to trauma. The meaning one makes of the abuse and the pain it causes us is what turns abuse into trauma.

Abusive or traumatogenic (i.e., trauma-causing) events may involve deliberate acts of physical or sexual violence, or subtler, but just as damaging, acts of neglect, coercion, emotional abuse, and betrayal. Traumatogenic events are distressing events beyond the scope of normal human experiences that overwhelm our usual coping resources — examples include assaults, accidents, and natural disasters. All trauma arises from external events, whether these involve acts of *commission* (e.g., bullying, stalking, physical abuse) or acts of *omission* (e.g., neglect, the absence of a parent). A range of acts may be considered traumatogenic. Many traumatogenic acts in relationships are abusive in nature, as they involve one person deliberately inflicting hurt on another. People can also be traumatised by events that were not deliberately abusive, such as a car accident. We often use shorthand and talk about abuse as 'traumas' — in this book I will use the term trauma to refer both to harmful events and to their impacts.

It is easy to recognise when one has experienced a 'Big T' (life-threatening) trauma, such as a violent assault or injuries sustained in armed combat. 'Little t' (i.e., not life-threatening) traumas are subtler and often go unrecognised by the victims or people around them. The distinction between them has been driven largely by the need to delineate a possible life-threatening event for the purposes of diagnosis of post-traumatic stress disorder using DSM-V criteria. While we will discuss some Big T events in this book (sexual assault is an example), many of the traumas I discuss fit into the little t category.

When clients with relational abuse and trauma histories first come to therapy, they are usually confused about the nature of what they experienced, and often have not realised that their difficulties relate to trauma. Smaller, cumulative events can be easy to miss, or explain away.

Many trauma survivors are haunted by feelings of anxiety and perfectionism, and struggle to manage these difficulties using typical cognitive-based psychological treatments. This often compounds their distress, and they feel like a failure at therapy. Many of them have a sense that things have never been quite right. They often report that they have difficult relationships, can't find suitable partners, or partner up with people who hurt them. They may report that they shut off during sex, or have intense body hatred and difficulties with eating disorders. They carry incredibly high standards for themselves and are very punishing and demanding towards themselves when they do not achieve these standards. Sometimes, traumatised people notice that their lifestyles have a lot of chaos and that they move from job to job, or feel restless and move cities every couple of years, just as they are beginning to settle in somewhere.

Some of my clients have hurt other people in relatively serious ways and come to me through my work in forensic psychology. They sometimes acknowledge that they have hurt other people but almost always tell me stories of the deep harms that they faced at the hands of other people before they started hurting people themselves.

The initial work for many trauma clients involves recognising when a trauma history underlies their current troubles and then understanding the tasks of trauma recovery. This is often a challenging process, as people have many misconceptions about relational traumas. Here are some of the common ones I have heard.

'Some traumas are worse than others.'

'People cannot heal from childhood abuse.'

'Everyone with trauma gets PTSD.'

'She is anxious after being assaulted, so she must have PTSD.'

'You need to do X/Y/Z therapy to recover.'

'The person who abused me needs to own up to it before I can heal.'

'You need to forgive the person who hurt you before you can heal.'

'I will never feel better.'

In this chapter, I will address some of these myths, speak about the nature of different traumatic events, and tackle the common trajectories of post-traumatic recovery and the various points at which one might get stuck in recovery.

People often assume that experiences that do not involve

physical harm are less harmful than experiences that involve physical or sexual abuse. However, various forms of emotional abuse (e.g., manipulation, isolation, controlling behaviours, and name-calling) involve acts designed to reduce a victim's self-esteem, sense of safety, agency, or sense of belonging, and will have significant psychological impacts on their perception of self. Most of these acts fit under the umbrella of coercive control, i.e., patterns of abuse and harm designed to threaten, scare, intimidate, or punish someone. 'Coercive control' is a term used in the domestic violence literature and is similar to the psychological concept of emotional or psychological abuse. Psychological abuse can occur in all types of relationships, not just spousal/partner relationships.

Most complex trauma survivors will start therapeutic work by saying something along the lines of 'It wasn't that bad', or, 'I shouldn't be feeling like this, at least X [insert worst trauma one can think of] didn't happen.' I usually gently encourage them to reflect on the invisible measurement scale they carry in their head, and the notion that certain traumas are worse, or better, than others.

Minimising ('it could have been worse') is a very common response and an easy psychological defence against pain that might otherwise overwhelm. If something wasn't that bad, surely it is okay to tuck it away and forget about it, instead of paying attention to it? Sometimes the use of 'it wasn't that bad' comes from years of conditioning and training in being self-effacing and putting one's needs last (a common psychological pattern within families where there has been abuse or neglect), and sometimes it indicates a range of internalised beliefs that make recognising the true harm that has been done to one very difficult. When someone struggles with this embedded belief, I often ask them what they would say to their dearest friend, if their friend was to disclose carrying that same history. The only barometer a trauma survivor needs is their understanding of their own experience. There is no 'better' or 'worse' trauma to have. Everyone will react to events differently. Some of the differences in response may be based on the age at which the trauma(s) occurred, the person's natural temperament, the support around them at the time and since, their social capital (i.e., the assistance they can access), and their capacity to process and understand the trauma.

For instance, someone who experiences a sexual assault but has no prior abuse history, is well supported within a relationship, and can seek psychological support soon after the event is more likely to recover faster than someone with a prior history of sexual abuse, who is relatively mistrustful of other people, and is isolated and unemployed, therefore precluding them from accessing appropriate supports after the assault.

As a rule of thumb, I use the following 4Cs concept to help people understand the impact of a trauma. Regardless of the nature of the act perpetrated, traumatic events are likely to have greater psychological impacts if they:

- occurred in childhood (because this is a key developmental period, when we are laying down neural pathways and developing core beliefs about ourselves and the world);
- are chronic (i.e., occur repeatedly);
- are cumulative (i.e., may be compounding an earlier trauma); or
- affect a core part of someone's identity.

As one example, several of my clients present with histories of bullying at school or work and are perplexed about the strength of their responses to these events. They will often blame themselves, because 'it was just bullying, I should be over this by now'. When I use the 4Cs framework to help them explore it, they realise that bullying is chronic in nature, can be cumulative with other adverse experiences, and may strike at the heart of a core part of someone's identity — their vocational competence, in the workplace scenario.

Relationally traumatic events are those that are inflicted by other people, usually intentionally. When I say trauma, most people instinctively think of physical or sexual assault. In this book, we cast the net somewhat wider and look at a range of events that occur within the bounds of relationships, systemic structures, and families — and which may or may not involve deliberate physical harm. Interpersonal and complex trauma most often involves patterns of harmful behaviour, though standalone events of enough severity also occur.

Recognising traumatic events

It is important to note that not everything difficult that occurs in relationships is traumatic. We are all likely to have had parents who sometimes became angry with us; to have been rejected in relationships, spoken to harshly, or been betrayed by a friend; to have had fights that involved raised voices, and experienced rudeness at work. I do not want to pathologise these relatively normal experiences or suggest that we need to protect ourselves from everything aversive. Part of good psychological management involves recognising that we are not perfect and nor are other people. It's likely that we will encounter difficult relational experiences at various points — and will inflict them ourselves. Good psychological functioning involves the capacity to recognise and navigate these experiences and build resilience, so that they don't trouble us more than necessary. It could even be considered beneficial to have some difficult experiences (e.g., rejection, failure) so we can learn to process and manage difficult emotions. Usually, and ideally, we would be supported through this process by parents and caregivers, allowing us to develop good emotional management. However, without this support (such as if parents are neglectful) even simpler difficult experiences may overwhelm functioning and feel traumatic. And some experiences (such as sexual or physical assault, emotional abuse) clearly sit outside the boundaries of the manageable and are deemed traumatic and/or abusive.

It is difficult to provide a clear set of experiences that are traumatic versus those that are not. Often, the boundary that delineates traumatic from non-traumatic experiences is dependent on how the person involved in it experienced the event. On other occasions, interpersonal traumas occur not because of what happened to a person, but because of what *didn't* happen. All people have core physical and psychological needs: for food, warmth, shelter, stimulation, care and safety, belonging, acceptance, spontaneity, independence, and agency. When these needs are either not met or are thwarted in some way, what results is an assault on a developing self, which can manifest in trauma reactions. So when thinking of trauma, it is important to look not only for the presence of harmful experiences but also for the *absence* of positive experiences and nurturance.

The events that I would usually consider relationally traumatic include: sexual abuse or assault as a child or adult; physical abuse or assault as a child or adult; witnessing family violence as a child; emotional abuse or coercive control (i.e., a pattern of verbal abuse, belittling, name-calling, control, manipulation, denying your reality, or anger directed at you); being parentified (i.e., being asked to take on the emotional or physical tasks that a parent within the family usually would); neglect by a parent (i.e., not having emotional or physical needs reliably attended to); the sudden loss or death of a parent or sibling; bullying at school or work (especially if protracted, or if it occurs at key developmental stages); being stalked; abuse within an intimate relationship; a severe and sudden betrayal by someone close; and religious abuse/control, including joining a cult.

I want to note that sometimes trauma and abuse can occur within (or to) entire groups. Reflecting on growing up in India, it struck me that it is a culture characterised by a form of stark coercive control directed at all women, perpetrated by almost everyone — families, schools, workplaces, religious and legal institutions, and the government itself. This was couched in terms of 'morality' and 'family values', but the emphasis was on repressing and controlling female agency, behaviour, sexuality, and bodies. Traumas and abuse such as child sexual abuse, rape, and domestic violence were implicitly facilitated by the cultural norms. Other aspects of the culture were also really problematic, such as the rampant poverty, corruption, and abuse of power by the rich. While I cannot cover experiences of group-harm in this book because the scope is too vast, I can acknowledge them and remind readers to be aware of societally sanctioned forms of abuse, such as racism.

Sometimes, relational traumas can take the form of a bad temperamental fit between caregiver and child (e.g., a very shy child with an outgoing parent), such that the child feels isolated within the family or learns to believe that they are unacceptable. Over time, the micro-rejections experienced within this situation are tantamount to an experience of relational trauma, exerting powerful influence over the beliefs the child will likely form about themselves, and the resultant shame they will likely feel. That said, some people will experience some of the events I have listed above and recover without experiencing specific post-traumatic difficulties, especially if they experience these events on a background of stability and consistency in early life.

Identifying and responding to traumatic events

Typically, when a significant traumatic event (e.g., a violent assault at work) occurs in adulthood, there is an immediate recognition of the nature of the event and the psychological consequences that may follow. Support is often provided to someone who experiences this type of event to manage and monitor how they feel after it. Victims are offered space to debrief, and there is peer and family support. There is a normalisation of the trauma response process, and an understanding that victims are likely to experience a range of difficult feelings and demonstrate some trauma-related behaviours (e.g., nightmares, irritability). All these processes facilitate recovery as people cohere together against the harms done.

Relational trauma can bring some very specific difficulties, and the first of these is that the event may not be recognised as traumatic until much later. Certain types of interpersonal abuse start very subtly (e.g., coercive control in intimate relationships) and the nature and effects of these events are often not recognised until the victim has been able to leave the situation. And there are other traumas that can remain unidentified by the victim — or people around them — at the time of the incident. Sexual assault is a common example: some sexual experiences may be normalised in certain contexts (e.g., being groped, sexual intercourse without explicit consent with a partner), or may not be labelled as traumatic by the victim until much later. There is still a huge amount of stigma and shame around being sexually offended against, so many victims, even though they recognise and label the offense, don't seek support or disclose the trauma. When trauma experiences are repressed, they tend to fester. Stalking is similar, in that it often goes unrecognised both by victims and the people around them. Stalking behaviour terrifies victims because of the level of intrusion into their lives. Victims often feel great anxiety, though they may struggle to link it to the intrusions they faced and may not realise that they were stalked until years later, typically labelling the stalker as someone 'persistent' or 'annoying'. Without recognition of harmful acts, people do not know that they can seek support.

Sometimes, events are deliberately mislabelled by perpetrators, with victims told repeatedly that abusive behaviour is normal or innocent. Powerful examples of these types of events include: childhood sexual abuse ('I am doing this to show you my love'); emotional abuse ('you made me do this'); coercive control ('I only followed you to make sure you got to work safely, why are you overreacting?'); bullying ('I am only giving you feedback, you must just not be up to the job'); or intimate partner violence ('you made me angry because you came home late, it's your fault I hit you'). These events, and the behaviours of people who perpetrate these actions or systems around the victim, make it especially difficult for victims to *a.* recognise, *b.* name and address the abusive behaviour, and *c.* externalise blame and anger to the perpetrator, instead of feeling shame and guilt. The latter — being able to place blame and responsibility — is extremely important as it allows emotions such as anger to be processed and directed where they belong, which can mean that the emotional intensity reduces with time.

People who experience these forms of abuse often report that it started in less severe ways, making it difficult to identify the precise starting point. For instance, most childhood sexual abuse survivors report that boundaries are slowly breached, and the abusive acts escalate over time. This can mean that the victim becomes accustomed to some of these behaviours and identifies them as their 'normal' instead of noticing that they are abusive — think of the 'frog boiling in pot of water' analogy. For childhood sexual abuse victims, they may recall that initially they found themselves alone with the perpetrator, then experienced non-intimate touching (such as tickling), before this escalated even further. This is also common with intimate partner abuse or bullying, where the abuse may commence with less severe acts (e.g., yelling during an argument) that then escalate into physical violence or control.

Another important factor in someone's capacity to recognise abuse is the perpetrator's patterns of behaviour. Many perpetrators of relational trauma will also provide a victim with love, support, and positive reinforcement at various times as part of the structure of the relationship. This often results in the victim choosing to forgive the episodes of abuse or simply not noticing them, because the broader backdrop of the relationship is one where they perceive closeness and care from the perpetrator. This is commonly described in the 'cycle of violence' used to explain intimate partner violence, demonstrating a slow build-up, an explosion, expressions of regret, reparation, and love — until the cycle commences afresh. This cycle is not always intentional and tailored. Perpetrators may feel sorry and try to stop their abusive behaviours but fail because they don't understand what causes them, and thus don't know how to change them.

Expressions of regret and love are especially difficult for victims to understand and marry with the reality of abuse, especially when they might want desperately to believe that a perpetrator loves them and will change. 'How can s/he hurt me, but also tell me that s/he loves me?' is a common question.

Some victims simply have no choice but to accept abuse — children who are emotionally, physically, or sexually abused by a caregiver are also often entirely reliant on the caregiver for nurturance, and it is almost psychologically and physically unsurvivable for a child to accept that the person who loves and cares for them also hurts them.

Traumas that remain unrecognised and unlabelled by the victim and the systems around the victim ensure that no support is offered to the victim, and that normal recovery processes (such as debriefing and seeking support) are not accessible. I want to be clear here that stating this is not the same as victim-blaming. Perpetrators often actively ensure that a victim does not recognise they are being abused; certain types of abuse are very subtle and not well addressed in the common lexicon; and many powerful systems, institutions, and cultures are set up to hide abuse and protect perpetrators — such as the way the Catholic church moved paedophile priests between dioceses. This behaviour isn't relegated to the past — looking at the way certain sections of the media rush to protect powerful men accused of abuse reminds me that we have a lot of work to do.

Common post-traumatic symptoms can take on a few forms. Many trauma clients notice *cognitive* alterations (i.e., changes in how they think). Common examples include:

'I can't stop thinking about what happened.'

'I can't concentrate anymore.'

'I worry all the time.'

'I often think that people are going to hurt me.'

'I think that everything is my fault.'

Other common responses include *affective* responses (i.e., symptoms related to how someone feels, such as being anxious or hypervigilant). Difficult emotions may include feelings about the traumatic event itself, such as horror, anger, fear, or sadness, but will also likely encompass changes in feelings in daily life. This can include experiencing more intense feelings than usual, having feelings that change rapidly, or feeling more numb, irritable, hopeless, or sad than usual. Some people experience changes in behaviour (e.g., social withdrawal or sleep problems).

All of these are *normal* symptoms trauma survivors experience and are a way for the brain and body to find rest after a trauma, to create a narrative and explain the event, protect oneself, and integrate what happened with one's worldview and set of beliefs. These symptoms become problematic when they continue for too long. The DSM-V states that someone meets the criteria for a diagnosis of PTSD when their symptoms last for more than one month.

We all have different baselines for our moods, thoughts, and behaviours, so it's helpful to identify changes to a usual baseline when trying to understand post-traumatic changes. This process is likely to be very difficult for survivors of childhood abuse, because childhood abuse usually means that someone's entire personality and way of being may have been shaped by the trauma, and it is often difficult to determine a pre-morbid (i.e., before the injury) baseline. With clients who have experienced child abuse (whether emotional, physical, or sexual), I tend to look for thought patterns or feelings that are especially difficult to manage or harmful to functioning.

For instance, Suzie's hyper-independence, her reserve, and her strong feelings of defectiveness were formed very early in childhood and had become integrated into her personality. We had no baseline to compare her against, but instead worked to understand when these patterns were most problematic for her so we could start to change them.

Broadly speaking, if someone is experiencing significant changes in mood, feelings, thinking patterns, or behaviours post-trauma, these are likely to be a trauma response. Ideally, these symptoms would resolve through allowing the release of the normal feelings one experiences after a trauma event (e.g., anger, fear, sadness), seeking support, receiving supportive feedback from others (e.g., 'of course that wasn't your fault, you handled it the best you could'), and debriefing. All these experiences and changes are very normal after a traumatic event, and progressing forwards (and sometimes backwards) through them is a normal part of the healing process.

When do we get stuck in trauma recovery?

There are several ways in which we get stuck in the recovery process. As discussed earlier, when events are not labelled as traumas at the time they occur, and the usual supports and debriefing do not eventuate, these events may be denied altogether. They can be or ignored and repressed (i.e., pushed away, out of consciousness) and left to fester, until a triggering event activates the memory, and the survivor has a strong trauma-based response to a relatively innocuous occurrence. Suzie noticed that she often had a strong surge of fear when someone used the words 'not good enough'. She said that her mother used this phrase a lot and it quickly triggered a strong emotional response, as her helplessness and fear were suddenly activated.

I often use the analogy of an open wound with my clients. A trauma is a psychological wound — how do you think a physical wound would heal if you did not attend to it, but ignored it and carried on with business as usual? It would possibly get infected, but even if it didn't, there would likely be significant pain, and more scar tissue than if you had sought treatment at the time.

Relational wounds that occur in childhood will typically shape someone's entire identity and the ways they think and feel, leading to a range of problems that start very early in life, generally go unrecognised, and compound as life progresses. Anxiety is a good example: it often occurs post-trauma as an entirely understandable means of noticing and responding to threat, but over time can become ingrained in one's personality and can generalise to a wide range of situations, leading to people either avoiding those situations or, conversely, trying to compensate by over-functioning and thus experiencing great stress. In some cases, it may even lead to someone developing an avoidant personality structure (i.e., avoiding numerous things out of a fear of rejection), or social/generalised anxiety. Avoidance caused by anxiety reinforces and strengthens many post-traumatic symptoms, and can lead to increasing loops of avoidance and distress.

I often find in my work that trauma survivors have created a range of unstated beliefs about the events by the time they enter therapy (e.g., 'I made this happen because I could not protect myself', 'It happened because I was too weak to say no') and these beliefs can keep them stuck in difficult feelings such as shame and guilt. Many of my sexual assault clients present with these beliefs — and a lot of internalised self-blame about an act that was inflicted upon them and over which they realistically had no control. Sometimes people who have had relatively safe lives have beliefs around invulnerability (e.g., 'If I do the right thing, I will be fine', or 'Good things happen to good people, and bad things happen to bad people'). When a trauma happens, these beliefs can be blown apart, leaving the survivor scrambling to make sense of the world. People may re-form their beliefs post-trauma in unhelpful ways, such as 'if bad things happen to bad people, then I must have done something wrong to make this happen'. At other times, beliefs such as 'I don't need any help from others' can stop people from accessing supports after a trauma, leading to stalled recovery.

The initial core task of trauma recovery for many people is to unpick some of those beliefs, so that survivors can put the responsibility where it lies (with the perpetrators) and then move on with the tasks of addressing the difficulties the trauma has created. Sometimes, if we develop a set of problematic beliefs to explain why an event happened, they can subconsciously influence the way we behave. For instance, if one holds the belief that they were responsible for a sexual assault because they 'should have kept themselves safe', they are likely to second-guess their judgement or keep people at arm's length, and begin to notice difficulties with feeling socially disconnected, sad, and numb, thus compounding the effects of the initial trauma.

Overall, people can become trapped in the process of relational trauma recovery because of the beliefs they hold about the events and themselves, the manner in which they have learnt to defend against the world, the defences they bring to bear, and the emotional processing that has been thwarted. Often, all these factors are reinforced by the absence of supportive others, and systems that solidify and congeal the trauma.

2

The Impacts of Complex Trauma and Betrayal

The first time I saw Madison, she stormed into the therapy room. I was sitting in a poky office in the prison, uncomfortably pressed into a corner, away from the door. This was the unit supervisor's office and had a desk, a computer, and two chairs, vaguely positioned to face each other. It was far removed from a typical therapy room, though was often utilised as such, as well as for many other purposes.

One of the maxims impressed upon me during my forensic training was the importance of ensuring that you have an escape route — always. Know where the door is, know where the duress button is, and *never* allow a client between the door and yourself.

Madison sat down on the chair closest to the door and stared at me, as though sizing me up. I would have preferred that she had been sitting where I was, away from the door, but the unit staff did not want her out of their line of sight. I weighed up a few things in my mind in a split second: the two doors, the few steps between the officer's post and where we were, and my dependence on their reliably watching us in an often busy protection unit.

People are placed in protection units within mainstream prisons when they need to be isolated from the broader compound for their own safety, either due to the nature of their offences, or because they have had interpersonal difficulties with co-prisoners, or other risk issues. While in protection, prisoners are contained to their unit 24 hours a day, only being allowed into the rest of the compound when the mainstream prisoners are locked in. This creates a maelstrom of difficulty: protection prisoners have little capacity to buffer themselves from any dynamics on the unit through engagement in other activities, such as exercise or attending work. It felt to me like a very antisocial high school, with multiple problems among the prisoners.

As Madison sat before me, I considered my knowledge of her offences, the lack of any recorded history of staff assaults, her intense need for therapy and clear desire to be there, the number of at-risk calls (i.e., when a client expresses suicidal thoughts) we had received over the preceding weeks, the intensity of her affect and gaze, and the comforting presence of the large duress button on my belt. 'You will be triangulated within half a metre, and people will be there in seconds,' I had been assured during induction, and I had ascertained that this was true when I accidentally hit my duress one time and had a swarm of correctional staff descend on me. It was reassuring, and I always felt safer in prison than I do out in the broader community. Of course, this safety came at the price of containment and control, even for staff.

Affect is commonly described as the outward expression of internally felt emotion. We generally assess a person's affect as an insight into their mental state (or how stable their current mental functioning is). We look for things like the type of affect (angry, fearful, anxious), the intensity, the congruence and appropriateness (e.g., is someone talking about something distressing, but laughing in an incongruent manner?), how reactive (i.e., responsive) someone is, and any deviations from the person's baseline. Intensity of affect can sometimes signal preoccupation with difficult emotions and may signal an increased risk of committing physical assault, and difficulties such as incongruent affect can often point to underlying mental illness. It is not typical for clients to assault clinicians, as there is a clear view that we are there to help, and people often retain a sense of that and the capacity to modulate their behaviour in response. Nevertheless, it is certainly not beyond the realm of possibility for clinicians to be assaulted, and there have been a few notable incidents within my own forensic teams.

I judged it unlikely that Madison would harm me and decided to proceed. The pragmatics of prison work in a poorly resourced system meant that I sometimes breached the rules I was taught — if I didn't, I would never have seen any clients because of space and time constraints.

'My partner broke up with me,' Madison barked, 'but it's okay, I don't care.'

She buried her head in her hands. She spoke in a staccato manner for ten minutes, switching between anger and apathy, and brushing past the edges of sadness. She was unable to hold one emotional state for more than a few seconds, and each time an emotion became strong, she retreated into a defence of 'It's okay, I don't care', or changed the subject, moving into a blithe description of dynamics on the unit or easier-to-tolerate discussions about difficulties with her friends. When I reflected that she seemed to be experiencing a mix of difficult feelings about the break-up, she abruptly stood up and asked to end the session.

Over the months we worked together, this intolerance of emotion would come to characterise my work with Madison. It manifested as intense difficulties accessing any internal state (i.e., thoughts or feelings), to the point where any encouragement to reflect on how she felt about something led to Madison asking to end the session. She was unable to notice conflicting feelings about anything, or to hold an integrated emotional experience, instead switching abruptly between the various selves she held. These selves were simply the various facets of her emotional experiences. Like most of us, she had different ways of experiencing emotion and behaving, sometimes appearing very detached, at most other times angry, and only very occasionally — vulnerable. Complex trauma survivors often have very distinct divisions between parts of their selves such that they may struggle to integrate these selves and can often feel like their experiences are uncontrollable (e.g., quickly flipping into an enraged part of their self). When taken to extremes, this is what gives rise to Dissociative Identity Disorder (formerly called Multiple Personality Disorder).

The language of 'parts' comes from certain therapies such as schema therapy and internal family systems (IFS) work. I often use schema therapy[1] in trauma work — it's very helpful with conceptualising and amending some of the broad belief structures that people form after interpersonally traumatic events, or when people have strong reactions related to the different parts of their self, as Madison did. Schema therapy posits that people have a range of childhood needs. When any or all of these needs remain unmet, people develop a range of beliefs, emotional responses, and coping mechanisms and behaviours (i.e., schemas) which become habitual, and colour one's view of oneself and all of one's behaviours and interactions with the world. These schemas can also manifest in what psychologists call 'modes', or the parts of self described below.

Modes are really just ways people act out their schemas in the world, and all the thoughts and feelings that arise in a situation as different schemas are triggered. An example of this in operation might be when someone with an abandonment schema feels ignored by a friend and flips into what we call an 'enraged child' mode (e.g., sending them a number of furious text messages and punching a hole in the wall), whereas another person with the same schema might experience the same feelings but instead drink a bottle of wine as a way of soothing and detaching from difficult feelings. We all respond to the world in characteristic ways based on our schemas, and how we have learnt to express them. Because trauma gives rise to so many unsettling beliefs about the world and oneself and such poor emotional regulation, schema therapy can be very powerful with understanding and amending habitual patterns.

Madison named her selves/modes the 'no fucks given' Madison, the 'sad child' Madison, and the 'blank' Madison. Fundamentally, she could not understand and express her own mental state (also called 'mentalising') because of the overwhelming emotion she often felt. This emotion was a boiling mass and usually, she just noticed that she felt angry. This is a common response for many trauma victims, especially those who learnt early that emotion would be ignored or punished, and that stoicism and detachment were more effective at avoiding punishment. Madison had learnt early to pay no attention to how she felt, and she now struggled to tune into herself. Anger was the only emotion that felt safe to feel.

She spoke about her early life — in as much detail as she could tolerate — and about the unimaginable harms she had faced at the hands of everyone tasked with caring for her. We noted that her only means of understanding and managing any of these difficult times had been to shut down completely, to turn her loathing inwards, to adopt a tough and scary persona, and to use drugs to numb herself.

Madison was insightful and bright. She knew that some of the paths she had taken were very unhelpful, and she experienced internal conflict between her desire to change and have more for herself and her tendency to default to her usual coping mechanisms. I liked her and wanted to help her — which was interesting to me. While the likeability of a client doesn't correlate with the effort I make to help them, it *does* speak to the reaction they might evoke in other people, and to the dynamics I can draw on in the room. It is not possible to like every client, especially within the forensic setting, but I always aim to at least have unconditional neutral regard for every client,[2] and to find something I can like, or empathise with, in each of them. It is, however, interesting to realise I have been able to find something likeable in most of my clients, regardless of what they have done. Seeing the entirety of a person and tuning into their vulnerabilities naturally brings a deep care. It felt to me as if many people recognised the tightly guarded vulnerability in Madison, and custodial staff were supportive and as encouraging of our work as they could be, despite the complexity of her behaviours on the unit.

Our task together, initially, was to allow and build tolerance of her emotional experiences, so she did not react with rage, directed at herself (or other people), when she experienced something distressing. The experiences of her early life had resulted in both her overwhelming emotion, and her difficulties accessing and tolerating that emotion — her emotional door was welded shut.

We needed to crack open the door and allow her to safely experience emotions in my presence, so we could eventually open the door fully and explore the plethora of difficulties she faced, including her grief and losses, her anger and rage, and her knowledge of the warped form her life had taken, and how it might be made different and fresh.

Defences: the primary trauma management mode

When we think about traumatic events and the manner in which they influence people's understanding of the world, the first word that springs to mind is 'defence'.

Relational trauma is fundamentally an overwhelming series of events that sends a tsunami of emotion over our normal coping mechanisms, flooding us, psychologically speaking, and eradicating the sense of self we have either constructed or are just beginning to construct. To protect oneself and manage the trauma, the mind must create a set of defences against overwhelming pain. It might be easiest to conceive of this as a dike, a giant wall built to protect the mind and the self from knowledge of the harms done. This is especially salient when we consider the 'who' and the 'how' of relational traumas — often carried out by those close to us, and inflicted repeatedly, at critical developmental stages. To understand and survive an interpersonal trauma, we often need to wall it off and to wall off the emotions associated with it. In concert with this, we also develop a range of compensatory and defensive beliefs (e.g., 'I must be bad for my mother to treat me in that manner'). Many of these beliefs are entirely unconscious.

Psychological defences refer to the ways we protect ourselves against anything that might overwhelm or distress us. We all have defence mechanisms; they are common and highly adaptive. For instance, if we were to carry in mind the essential truth that we will all die someday, and that humanity is likely to wink out like a star when the sun dies (if not before), many of us would curl up in horror and become overwhelmed. Various defences help us manage this knowledge, including sheer denial and trying to achieve immortality through work or procreation (i.e., if our legacy lives on, we will never truly die).

When relational trauma is experienced, several key defences come into play to protect us. While these psychological defences are initially powerful and protective, over time they can stop people from understanding and processing the trauma, resulting in a raft of post-traumatic difficulties. These defence mechanisms can also become iatrogenic (i.e., harmful) as they generalise and creep into other areas of life, stunting psychological growth so that we are unable to fully access any of our emotions, or warping our belief structures. Denial can be protective when it is the bulwark against being overwhelmed by knowledge of childhood sexual abuse, but it is less adaptive when it becomes characterological (i.e., habitual and part of our personality) and protects us from recognising basic emotional cues, such as unhappiness within an intimate relationship, or harmful friendships.

We can think of the dike as a psychological wall that often springs leaks, and as we stand with our fingers jammed into the wall to stop the flood of overwhelming distress, we remain unable to move away from the wall. This keeps us trapped there, desperately protecting ourselves from the terrors that lie beyond, despite our desire to tear ourselves away.

Trauma is, fundamentally, a state of remaining frozen in time, pressed against the traumatic event, and the exhaustive need to maintain psychological defences is the primary mechanism that underpins it.

The most common psychological defence we utilise against difficult events or feelings is denial. Denial is simple: it is the equivalent of saying 'no, that didn't happen', or 'it happened, but it didn't hurt me'. It is one of the most primitive (i.e., formed early in development) defences; most of us will have utilised it as a child when asked if we have done something we don't wish to confess to. Perhaps instinctively, we say no, and maintain that stance, despite the damning evidence of a trail of cookie crumbs leading to us. Similarly, we use the defence in a range of ways against trauma; by denying it occurred, by denying that it had an impact on us, or by selectively denying parts of it.

Survivors often struggle to remember traumatic events. This can be attributed both to the difficulties with memory formation around emotionally distressing events[3] and to the psychologically defensive processes of 'forgetting' to protect against distress. Our brains do not encode emotionally distressing events into long-term memory successfully, such that we might only have 'flashes' of memory or remember certain senses (e.g., what we hear), and forget the rest. This process of poor memory encoding during trauma is often exploited by defence barristers when cross-examining sexual assault victims who cannot fully remember the details of their assault, because their brains were acting in self-protective ways.

Occasionally, I have worked with people who have stated that certain triggers (olfactory triggers are common, due to the links between the olfactory nerves and memory centres of the brain) suddenly evoke memories in greater detail than previously recalled. Working on processing trauma slowly, by talking about it in therapy sessions, can work in equally successful ways, as it allows clients to break past their initial defences and start to acknowledge the impacts of traumatic events or even to recall hitherto unexplored memories. This process is psychologically challenging, and most therapists work very carefully on pacing, to ensure that a client is not psychologically flooded with distress before they have built the capacity to tolerate that distress. Of course, clients cannot remember that which they have never encoded, and I am careful never to engage in techniques such as hypnosis to 'retrieve' forgotten memories, or to force any memory retrieval. These kinds of techniques are ethically very problematic and may sometimes lead to people retrieving false memories,[4] or confabulating (i.e., the brain automatically creating memories, though without any intention to deceive) under pressure. This phenomenon is what drove the satanic ritual abuse panic of the 1980s in America.

Other defence mechanisms include those that support trauma survivors to manage the overwhelming *feelings* that can come up. The most common defences against emotion are repression, suppression, and sublimation (i.e., either pushing emotion away and detaching, or converting socially unacceptable impulses, emotions, or behaviours into those that are socially sanctioned). Trauma clients often struggle to feel any emotion, or explain that they survived the harm by blocking out parts of it or ignoring the distress that came after. Dissociative experiences can occur when traumas are overwhelming or happen at a certain developmental stage, essentially allowing the survivor to psychologically detach from the uncontrollable distress that can arise. This can take the form of full-blown dissociation, where difficult experiences and emotion are walled off into personality fragments, resulting in Dissociative Identity Disorder (DID) or other dissociative disorders, or in subtler ways, such as going 'numb' whenever a painful feeling intrudes, or collapsing and going to bed for a few days after a triggering event. I have worked with trauma survivors who have experienced functional psychogenic seizures (i.e., seizures caused by the functioning of the nervous system, not organic difficulties with the structure of the brain) when they have encountered any reminders of the traumatic event. Some clients describe watching themselves from above as they think of trauma memories. Dissociation is a part of healthy psychological functioning at times — we all need to cut off from emotion to function in various spaces (or go on autopilot while driving) — but is problematic when it walls off intense emotion that is then neither allowed out nor processed.

Many survivors seek deliberate ways of numbing emotion, including substance use and self-harm, such as cutting/hurting oneself. Pain can elicit endorphins, which can serve to snap a survivor back to the present and away from a difficult past experience, and is often instinctively utilised by people who struggle to hold and tolerate emotion.[5] It's also common for trauma victims to channel instinctive emotional responses into more socially acceptable pathways, such as channelling intense anger and distress into a desire to help other people as a means of making the bad beautiful, or into activism in the trauma field. Neither of these activities are inherently problematic — they're noble pursuits in and of themselves — but channelling unprocessed and unacknowledged emotions into the act of caring for other people can have emotional consequences both for the survivors and the people in their care.[6]

The 'wounded healer'[7] is a well-known trope in the mental health, social services, and medical fields. Some people with certain psychological histories and temperaments are drawn to the healing professions — to find healing and succour, as well as to prevent the harms they suffered being inflicted on others.

Of course, we can't control what happens to other people, despite our best efforts, and we absolutely *cannot* heal ourselves only through the vessel of helping others. The complex challenges of recognising and accepting one's limits, and managing intense workloads, difficult clients, our own wellbeing, and psychological processing often throw up a range of challenges for anyone working in the health and social welfare fields, let alone a trauma survivor. Trying to heal oneself by moving into healing other people can be disastrous, both for us and for them.

Another common defence mechanism is reaction formation: replacing a distressing feeling, urge, or thought with the opposite behaviour. Children who have been victimised by their parents are often unable to acknowledge their parents as harmful and at fault, because the dissonance of knowing that the person responsible for caring for them is the one who harms them is too much to bear. Sometimes abused children become intensely bonded to the abusive parent, in a compensatory mechanism for the distress and anger buried within the child, and as a form of allying with the parent to keep themselves safe. The child's anger towards the parent may become too strong to be allowed into conscious awareness, pushing the child closer to the parent as a mechanism of reassuring themselves that the parent is loving and safe, even as they repress their own feelings.

A range of other defences concern how abuse victims relate to the world and to other people. Projection and displacement are common and involve displacing difficult emotion from the original source to a less troubling source. I have known people who have experienced sexual abuse in childhood and who direct their rage not at the perpetrators, but instead at non-offending family members (usually parents) who were unable to protect them. It often feels safer and more useful to rage at parents, especially if the initial perpetrator is unavailable. While I do not absolve parents of all responsibility and there are some parents who deliberately turn a blind eye and are thus complicit in the abuse, many parents are genuinely unaware and/or have their own defences, including denial. While rage at non-offending family can superficially appear useful and healthy, over time it can serve to maintain emotional distress, because the parents cannot fix that which they did not cause. The unrelieved anger may further separate the trauma survivor from the supports available to them, strengthening even further an isolation that is already keenly felt.

Projection involves pushing qualities and attributes we dislike or are uncomfortable with onto other people. Trauma survivors are often made deeply anxious by anger and want to avoid it at all costs. Internally experienced anger is projected onto other people, such that the survivor may perceive other people as angry or hateful, while maintaining their own psychological defences against what they perceive to be a dangerous emotion. Projection itself can be dangerous, though, as it allows one to demonstrate denial of one's own psyche; anything unacceptable is projected outward, which can lead to a moral rigidity that engenders harmful behaviours (e.g., if we feel that only we are right and that other people are monsters, we can do what we wish to them).

Another defensive process is identification: where someone identifies deeply with another person and some of their behaviour and traits. Most of us learn by mirroring from other people; in this sense, identification is a normal developmental process. It can, however, become problematic when we absorb traits from those who perpetrate harm or if we rely on identification with significant others as a means of building an identity. My forensic clients often report that they had people in their lives who modelled aggression and anger for them, long before they engaged in these behaviours themselves. Many of my clients notice that they identified with the perpetrator of this aggression (often the same-sex parent) and unconsciously started mirroring some of the behaviours they witnessed in childhood, even if they consciously rejected the aggression that coloured their early years.

Other common defence mechanisms can involve avoidance of emotions or situations, the unconscious conversion of emotional distress into somatised symptoms (i.e., showing emotions through illnesses such as pain), the use of humour, and splitting (i.e., rigid black and white thinking where things are either good or bad, without being integrated into a whole). Many trauma survivors have a wickedly dark sense of humour, and this can be adaptive to a certain point — it's okay to laugh about the difficult things that have happened to us, if we don't too frequently use this just to avoid pain.

Defence mechanisms are not inherently problematic if *situationally dependent* and if we have some insight into how and why these defences operate. In one of the great double binds of psychological functioning, defences usually operate at a level outside our conscious awareness, rendering the task of noticing them challenging. Defences can become problematic if they become so ingrained in our psychological functioning that they develop into a consistent and natural part of operation — effectively becoming part of our personality and stopping us from consciously considering situations and making choices. We've all known people who quickly flip into denial when something difficult happens, 'no, it's fine, I just need to think positively', or those who refuse to see the bad behaviour of other people, 'it's okay, he promised he would change'.

It would be remiss to discuss relational traumas and defence mechanisms without addressing the role of shame. Fundamentally, shame involves a deeply felt sense of 'I am bad' (distinct from guilt — 'I have done something bad'). Relational traumas involve a large amount of shame, developed through a few mechanisms: clear messages communicated by perpetrators and systems, and multiple moments of lack of attunement with caregivers, which can communicate to a child the message that they are somehow at fault for having the self they do, or having the needs they are expressing. Many psychological defences arise to protect one from the knowledge of this shame.

Often, the traumas themselves become a point of shame, as the survivor knows that the traumatic events are in some ways abnormal, without a clear understanding as to why. This sense of shame can become part of a person's psyche, which can render the world a deeply distressing set of experiences of rejection. Managing shame requires a solid understanding of the relational basis of this shame, and close connection with a few non-shaming, accepting, and attuned others. While conscious self-talk and cognitive work can be beneficial, the remedies for shame most often lie in experiencing implicit, repeated acceptance from close others until this acceptance can be felt by someone, *for* oneself.

Trauma responses: fight-flight-freeze-tend and befriend

When a trauma occurs, or danger is perceived, the most common neurobiological responses involve fighting (whether literally or metaphorically), fleeing the danger, or freezing, as a mechanism of protecting against pain. We all have biological predispositions to responding in a certain way, and the magnitude of the perceived danger and our perception of the risk of harm will also affect our response. These mechanisms are out of our conscious awareness and occur in a split second — consider the experience of jumping when startled. You would likely have reacted quickly, even as you registered the surprise, with no space or time for conscious processing.

Responses to relational traumas utilise the same neurobiological pathways and people may fight, flee, or freeze, depending on their temperament, the nature of the trauma, and the type of harm the perpetrator is threatening. Victims often hold guilt about the way they responded ('I should have fought back') — and indeed, this messaging is reinforced by the world ('Why didn't she fight back?'), despite the well-established nature of our split-second trauma appraisal and response, and the biological basis of these responses.

Sometimes, the mechanisms of fight, flight, or freeze can become personality-driven learned features, such that people will characteristically respond to *any* threat with anger and aggression (fight); or by avoidance of any perceived danger (flee); or by detachment, dissociation, and surrender (freeze). Ideally, when responding to a non-immediate danger or threat, we want to retain the capacity to carefully evaluate the situation and determine the most adaptive and useful response.

Post-traumatic psychological difficulties can occur when survivors are unable to exercise a choice over their responses or to engage in conscious emotional processing of threats. Dissociation and freezing-based responses are especially difficult for survivors to manage and can evoke a lot of shame, as people question why they just didn't run away or fight back. While true tonic immobility (a reflexive lack of movement) is relatively rare, most freeze responses are underpinned by learned dissociation. Dissociative responses are a means of trying to detach from a painful experience to lessen the pain experienced — essentially taking psychological flight, usually into oneself. Dissociative tendencies can become hardwired into some survivors so that certain triggers or experiences of distress can immediately tip them into a space of feeling 'cut off' from the world and emotions.

Managing these responses can involve understanding the biological imperatives that underlie them, understanding why we respond in the way we do, and forgiving ourselves for the ways in which we may have responded to a traumatic event. Equally, if we find that our threat responses have generalised and we respond to even smaller threats by fighting, fleeing, or freezing, the work might involve slowly amending these responses, such as by learning grounding to help us freeze less often, or learning to approach smaller threats instead of fleeing.

'Tend and befriend'[8] is a different response. It is not a typical part of the literature on our basic biological responses to threat, but it's frequently discussed when talking about how women experience trauma or adversity. It involves providing care to other people and seeking social affiliation, largely as a means of garnering support. To put it bluntly — three women can fight off a man, whereas one woman likely cannot. The 'tend and befriend' response — sometimes called 'fawning' (i.e., engaging in people-pleasing behaviours) — at least partially derives from the socialisation women receive around being friendly and pleasant. It may also be a derivative of the freeze response, where it is easier and more adaptive to placate an abuser than to take the risk of fighting with someone clearly much stronger than oneself.

The survivors of sexual assault I have worked with often report some variant of this response, saying things like, 'I told him he was my friend', 'I said no, but politely', or 'he asked to come in, so I let him in'. There is huge guilt and shame in the way traumatised people perceive these responses as having contributed to the trauma; and of course, this is well exploited by the outraged cries of uninformed sections of the media ('Why was she friends with him?') and harsh cross-examination by defence barristers. This response is a difficult one to work through therapeutically because of the intense guilt involved, and often involves looking closely at what a motivated offender would likely have done if she *had* said no (my forensic experience comes in handy here) and uncovering the forces of socialisation inherent in someone having learnt that their greatest qualities lie in being polite, being kind, and saying yes.

Boundaries, practising saying no, and being firm (or even rude when warranted) are some of the key skills I work on with female victims, and there is good reason for this. Of course, this may apply to men too, though I have found that most men have not been socialised to be always polite and kind in the same manner.

Warped: understanding how trauma forms core beliefs about the world and self

Most trauma survivors come to therapy experiencing problems with how they relate to themselves, and problems in how they relate to other people and the world. This is a helpful concept to hold in mind through this book: when I say 'problems relating to self', the most common arenas impacted are identity, the ideas, beliefs, and expectations we have about ourselves, and correspondingly, the way we use emotions to navigate the world.

We all have a range of beliefs and expectations about the world, even though these are usually unspoken. These beliefs and expectations are often the basis of our identity and could be as simple as 'When I wake up in the morning, I will wake up in a safe and warm house and will eat breakfast in peace before going to work', all the way to more complicated constructs, such as 'If I don't do well at everything the first time I try things, I consider myself a failure'.

We have beliefs about who we are, about other people, our capacities, the future, and our needs and wants from life — and these beliefs affect how we feel, and what we do.

We form these beliefs in a range of ways; most of them are absorbed from interactions with caregivers, teachers, peers, and extended families, and by modelling (i.e., learning by watching someone else do). A lot of my forensic clients have great difficulty with basic things such as retaining work or attending appointments on time. This is not because they are 'lazy', but is more likely because they grew up in traumatised and chaotic families where they did not receive any modelling of basic things such as waking up for work at the same time every day, or scheduling appointments, and are thus unable to manage themselves enough to do so. We all have a range of habits for daily life, including patterns in the ways we think and feel, and trauma can warp these habitual ways of being.

For people who were raised in safe, healthy homes, and who had parents who were consistent and reliable, beliefs and expectations are likely to sound like: 'Life is largely predictable. I will be warm, fed, and clothed. The same things happen at the same times most days. People will take care of me when I need, and I can ask for help and support. I trust my parents and teachers. People like me and encourage me to do my best. I will have a good life, with steady work. I can try new things and have fun. Sometimes I won't do well at things, but that is okay. Sometimes people say no to me, and that is part of life. I like people and people like me.'

Consider instead the range of beliefs that Madison held at the start of therapy:

'I never know what will happen and need to prepare for things to change all the time. Nothing will stay the same. People will hurt me. People being kind to me is dangerous, because they are likely doing it so they can use me in some way. Men are especially dangerous, and I need to hurt them to protect myself. My only value to men lies in giving them sex. I may as well sleep with men who want sex with me, because I'll be forced to have sex anyway and at least if I agree I won't be injured. My own family seem to hate me, so I must be wrong or bad. It is dangerous to feel safe and relax. I need to watch myself and have my own back. Attack before being attacked. My life is going to be awful, and I will probably be dead by 30 so nothing matters anyway, may as well have some fun.'

Many of these beliefs were defensive and were designed to help her tolerate the knowledge of the harms done to her and to keep her safe from further hurts.

As a way of expressing and managing some of these unstated beliefs, Madison developed a sense of hypervigilance and anxiety about the world. She had a strong belief that the world was dangerous, and she developed a 'kill or be killed' attitude. She used substances to numb herself, and, in the absence of good modelling from caregivers, believed she was incapable of managing her emotions or life without these substances. She hated feeling relaxed and was unable to engage in any calming activity, such as yoga or meditation. Instead of doing any mindfulness work to ground her, I settled on throwing a ball back and forth to her — this seemed to work well as a physical way of helping her calm enough that we could talk. She tended to selectively spend time with people who would eventually hurt or betray her, because of tightly held beliefs that she was unworthy of more, feelings of hopelessness, and difficulties with differentiating between safe and unsafe people. Because of her lifestyle, she didn't really even have the chance to meet safe and prosocial people. Over time, these beliefs and lifestyle decisions led to cycles of revictimisation and retraumatisation, further reinforcing her initial beliefs.

When considering the impact of trauma on beliefs about the world, it is important to be aware of whether someone started life with a set of realistic and helpful beliefs or whether they experienced traumas early in childhood that may have skewed their initial belief systems towards the unhelpful or rigid. Generally speaking, if abuse occurs early in life (a specific cut-off is difficult to provide, but I would suggest anything that occurs before the age of 12–13), it is likely to mean that people will form warped belief structures, and that the work of belief reformation will involve *understanding and then disrupting* those structures. If the traumatic event occurred later in life (e.g., bullying at work, intimate partner violence), and against a generally safe early-childhood backdrop, then the work is more likely to entail understanding how the traumas *conflicted with and changed* initial belief structures, and focusing on reformation of a healthy and realistic set of post-traumatic beliefs.

As a general guideline, a useful set of beliefs should be *realistic* (i.e., based on reality, not on our anxiety or opinions about an event), *flexible* (i.e., change over time or between situations), *helpful* (ie., support us to engage in the world and pursue what we desire) and *not absolute* (i.e., no all-or-nothings or musts). Victims often develop absolute beliefs ('I should always keep people at arm's length') that are not situation-dependent or responsive, and these beliefs can translate to a range of problematic behaviours and emotional difficulties, and eventually underpin the development of mental health issues.

I have described some common patterns of belief below, based on my training in schema therapy.

Not-good-enough

This schema is very common, often arising from a range of experiences where someone was told that they were not good enough or was blamed and punished for not achieving enough. These patterns can occur in families characterised by emotional abuse and can lead to people developing a deep-seated sense of failure, worries about underachievement, and strongly demanding or punishing critical internal voices.

Some people surrender to these beliefs and accept them as truth, and never try to achieve anything; other people push against them relentlessly, trying to prove the opposite point by overachieving.

This schema can include pervasive worries about achievement, shame about oneself, body image difficulties, hyper-competitiveness, constantly comparing oneself with others and finding oneself wanting, never being satisfied with achievement, repeatedly changing the goalposts, setting overly high standards for self and others, self-sabotage when things are going well, refusal to commit to anything (in case this leads to failure), anger when requests are made, and underachievement.

People will hurt me or leave me

At the root of this set of beliefs is the expectation that people will be unpredictable, cruel, and vicious, or, alternatively, that one will be abandoned and left by people. This belief can express itself in subtle ways: behaviour designed to push people away; leaving relationships prematurely (i.e., leave before one gets left); being hyper-alert to any signs of abuse or rejection; difficulties with commitment; seeking fault in people; 'testing' people; difficulties being alone; or, paradoxically, surrendering to the idea that one will inevitably be hurt by other people and so refusing to maintain boundaries or to assess people before plunging into relationships. These schemas are often strongly underpinned by attachment styles (discussed further in Chapter 3).

No one will ever meet my needs/ I am always alone

At the core of this belief is the struggle to recognise one's own needs, physical or emotional, and difficulty trusting that anyone else will be able to meet them. People who have this set of beliefs often report that they feel a deep sense of aloneness or a pit inside, such that no amount of care is ever enough. This belief can arise when caregivers are not present or are preoccupied (e.g., when parents are unwell, or a sibling is very sick and absorbs most of the attention in the house), or if caregivers or other close relationship partners are cold and withholding.

People with this schema may fear abandonment, being 'too much' for other people, being a burden, or being left alone. This can be a difficult experience to navigate — people often pre-emptively shut themselves off from the care that they seek, or they seek so much support and closeness that they overwhelm people, and thus experience the feared rejection.

I have to be perfect

'Perfectionism' is common to some relational trauma survivors. This pattern is likely to occur if the initial traumas involved caregivers who were very demanding and punitive (think, expectations of high grades and perfect behaviour) or involved people later in life (such as partners) who were very critical and blaming. Sometimes perfectionism develops as a response to anxiety in the aftermath of trauma ('If I am perfect and everything is just-so, then I am in control of my world'). For some survivors, this manifests as a focus on controlling the minutiae of one's life, such that people develop very rigid habits, and experience severe anxiety when these routines and structures are threatened. It is closely tied to the belief that one is not good enough and can sometimes operate as a defensive reaction to deep feelings of shame and inadequacy.

Perfectionism can manifest in a range of ways, from the overt, such as worrying about making mistakes or anxiety when trying something new, to the more subtle. Subtle signs of perfectionism may include: over-planning before starting something new (I have worked with clients who spend so long planning new ventures that they become paralysed by all the options); procrastination driven by worries about failure and difficulties tolerating the imperfect; focusing on the idea of 'failure' instead of allowing new experiences; an over-emphasis on needing things to be a certain way or finding the 'best' solution (most of our decisions and choices probably don't matter as much as we think they do); and trouble starting new projects.

I am helpless/My life is out of my control

Sometimes people who have been traumatised develop what is known as 'learned helplessness': they become used to being victimised and may believe that life and situations are out of their control, so they stop trying to effect change. A lack of control over one's life sits at the root of many psychological difficulties and can contribute to cycles of revictimisation.

Sometimes relational trauma involves very chaotic situations — such as when caregivers use substances and move around a lot — so survivors may be used to a level of chaos and have no sense of agency in their lives. At other times, caregivers or partners may be highly controlling, leaving someone with limited life skills and a belief that they are unable to do things for themselves. Regardless of the cause, this set of beliefs can manifest as underachievement, inability to commit to a course of action or to complete projects, and complete dependence and reliance on other people. Over time, people might notice that their anxiety and helplessness increase and generalise, so that things they used to do before now feel out of their reach.

I don't matter as much as other people

Relational trauma often involves exertion of power by one person over another, whether it is a parent exerting influence over a child or one partner coercing another. At the heart of most relationally traumatic events lies the imposition of one person's needs over the needs of another. Relational traumas often involve repeated implicit or explicit demands that the victim ignore their own emotional responses and needs (e.g., by being told not to cry, or not to seek support or tell anyone). Victims can internalise this template and learn to subjugate their own needs and sacrifice themselves for other people. It is also often highly adaptive for someone who is being abused to remain closely attuned to the perpetrator as a way of seeking safety ('If I can anticipate your needs and keep you happy, then you won't hurt me'), which can, in turn, lead to a lack of recognition of one's own needs.

In practice, this belief often means that survivors struggle to know what they want and need and may place other people ahead of them, choosing not to 'burden' other people with their needs and emotions, and taking a back seat in relationships. Over time, this can result in more distant relationships, or intense stress, as the survivor tries to meet everyone's needs and denies their own.

I don't know who I am: difficulties with identity after trauma

Associated with inflexible, defensive, and problematic belief structures, trauma brings some distinct difficulties with how people typically relate to and experience the world. When I say 'relate to the world', I am referring to the identities and habits people form as well as the way they express their values through their behaviours. 'Identity formation' is a mysterious term often used in psychology, and you have probably heard it used in relation to trauma.[9] People frequently describe trauma survivors as having a 'broken' or 'shattered' sense of self or having difficulties with identity cohesion.

To break this down a little — when we talk about identity, we mean the view people have of themselves, their personality traits, the values they hold dear, the things they like and dislike, and their aspirations, goals, and dreams — and some cohesion in all these things. The process of forming a clear identity often extends well past adolescence and into one's twenties. An identity involves the sum of one's psychological being — the unique constellation of traits, beliefs, defences, difficulties, strengths, and identifications that make up a person. It is formed through a complex and iterative process of nature and nurture, as an individual builds on their base temperament through experiences in the world.

Typically, by late adolescence, we expect people to have a semi-formed personality (i.e., stable attributes such as how extroverted someone is, how open they are to new experiences, and levels of conscientiousness, emotionality, and friendliness), a relatively stable gender and sexual identity — though it's also normal for these things to continue to shift as people explore them — and an initial idea of interests, values, and goals. The tasks in one's twenties are to explore the world, to solidify interests and goals, to temper personality traits (for instance, we tend to become less impulsive post-age 25, once the prefrontal cortex has fully matured), to create a better understanding of our values, and to develop better insight into issues such as partner and friend compatibility.

However, childhood trauma survivors sometimes experience some very specific and terrifying difficulties with developing and understanding identity. When there is abuse within the family or abuse at an early age, it can overwhelm a child's coping resources and direct attention away from the psychological processes of exploration, growth, adventure, and play towards simple survival. Sometimes, children are forced into roles in the family that shape their identity fully. An example might be a child who was parentified (i.e., forced to take on the emotional or physical tasks usually undertaken by a parent) and thus developed an identity based on self-sacrifice. Often, children who experience trauma are separated from their peers by design (i.e., it serves the perpetrator to keep them isolated so no one else notices the abuse) or accident (e.g., parents have chaotic lives and move a lot, so a child can never form friendships), and so they're unable to learn from their peers or to form identities aligned with the specific references within their peer group. I have trauma clients who were never allowed to watch television, because their controlling parents did not allow this, and so they were never exposed to the television shows that their peers were watching, couldn't contribute to any conversations about the shows, and found it difficult to develop an identity aligned with common cultural mores. While this might sound relatively insignificant, small separations mount and eventually coalesce to form the terrifying sense of isolation and separation carried by many relational trauma survivors. A similar process occurs when people experience coercive control in a relationship and are deliberately isolated from their peers and families.

Some types of abuse may involve tight limits on what people are able to do, see, or experience, stunting their capacity to explore the world and develop an identity (e.g., victims of intimate partner violence or coercive control not being allowed to spend time with friends, or to work). Often, people who are abused are very focused on the basic tasks of survival (not being hurt, managing their distress enough to continue functioning, placating the perpetrator) and don't have the emotional or intellectual space needed to explore the higher order questions of 'Who am I?' or 'What do I like?'. This is especially the case if the abuse occurred during key periods of identity formation, such as childhood and adolescence.

Some clients with trauma histories report that they don't have a sense of *any* identity — they can't articulate their favourite colour, for instance, and don't know what foods they like. Others notice rapidly shifting identities, such as suddenly changing their favourite food based on what their partner likes. Sometimes they feel panicked when their identities diverge from the identities/ wishes of people close to them, because it was dangerous for them to express a contrary opinion as a child. Some identity-shifting is normal — people influence us, and we want the capacity to take on new things over the course of our life — but we also want a general solid sense of knowing who we are, what we stand for, what we like and value, and what we dislike. Some trauma survivors simply don't have this, and they carry a very underdeveloped self into the world.

As a result of disruption to normal identity building, survivors can experience a range of difficulties related to how they engage with the world. Common ones include: difficulties relating to other people; trouble forming or keeping relationships and friendships; difficulties settling on or sticking to a career; trouble navigating change or making decisions; difficulties adhering to goals; trouble with planning and organisation (chaos in a person's life is the first clinical sign I look for when considering a history of relational trauma); problems with body image; sexual difficulties; and trouble implementing boundaries — many survivors are consistently taken advantage of by people around them, and some of this relates to behaviours they have normalised and learned to accept, or fears they hold about saying no.

3

The Trauma Survivor
in the World

I started seeing Anna when she was 33. She was seeking therapy to support her with the end of a difficult relationship. 'I think I'm falling apart,' she said, tight-lipped. I looked at her carefully; she appeared composed, but was twisting a tissue in white-knuckled hands. Rings of old ridged scars ran up her arm, signalling intense difficulties managing emotion and a history of self-harm as a way of soothing herself. There was a single fresh, angry scar slicing across her arm. Anna saw me looking at it.

'I tried to stop myself, but I just couldn't feel better. I wanted to die.' She started crying, softly at first and then furiously, sobs wracking her body. Over time, Anna told me her story, and we started to understand why the end of her relationship was so distressing that her own life ceased to hold meaning or value in comparison.

She spoke of her distant, withholding mother who was absorbed in her own pursuits and of being a young child left alone, desperately alone — even as she begged and pleaded to be loved and seen. She spoke of her angry father and the rages he would fly into, where he screamed at Anna and told her that she was disgusting and that no one would ever love her. She said that she hears his voice and feels petrified each time she feels a partner pulling away or rejecting her in any way. She said that she could not shake her father's voice from her internal landscape — that it went away when things were calm, but re-emerged as soon as she was wounded by a partner or close friend, and the small, shamed self, who had once felt so hated, reared her head. Anna preferred to be on her own, often refusing to connect with other people to avoid rejection, but then feeling deeply alone.

The world of a trauma survivor can be one of some confusion and fragmentation.

It involves a set of deep defences built to shield oneself from the knowledge of the trauma and the harms caused. These defences protect against the trauma, but they also protect against positive experiences — we cannot build a wall to keep out the sun without also blocking the light and the view. Anna had intimate knowledge of this — she hated feeling vulnerable and did her best to keep people at arm's length, preferring to have superficial relationships instead. While this sometimes protected her from rejection, it also meant that she had very limited social support to draw on, and often felt isolated and ashamed of being isolated, further strengthening the internalised, punitive voice of her father. When she *did* have relationships, she found it difficult to be reliably close to people; she yearned to merge with them, but also preferred to keep them at a firm distance, and she did a number of things that appeared almost self-sabotaging. She said it felt like there was an empty hole inside her, and nothing that partners did was ever enough to fill it.

'I would prefer to leave first; then at least I'm not waiting around for them to leave,' she once said.

This push-and-pull dynamic characterised our work together, often rearing into the therapy room as Anna pulled me closer, and then rebuilt her walls or abruptly cancelled sessions. Eventually, she ended therapy by simply disappearing after our last session without paying her outstanding fee and ignoring my attempts to contact her to settle this fee, and to rebook sessions.

This was not dissimilar to the self-sabotaging pattern she demonstrated in her other relationships.

Beyond the defences, the world of a trauma survivor involves a range of socio-cognitive difficulties: painful thought patterns, overwhelming feelings, intense anger, and a range of compensatory mechanisms to help manage or numb these difficult feelings, including patterns that appear self-defeating, such as deliberate self-harm or substance use. Some trauma survivors prefer to block out emotion completely, and often do so successfully for years by using a range of dissociative mechanisms. However, it is difficult to operate in the world with its attendant stressors without the guidance of one's emotions, and trauma survivors who resort to defensive emotional blocking often notice that they somatise emotions instead or that the blocking catastrophically breaks down, usually precipitated by stress. Other survivors have little emotional control, lashing out when any strong emotion arises, experiencing helplessness as they are flooded by difficult feelings. People can punish themselves for not living up to the rigid standards they hold, and they may punish others for the same sins.

The traumatised world is characterised by a deep sense of shame and defectiveness and a range of overcompensations for this, or, paradoxically, complete helpless surrender to that defectiveness. Lifestyle disorganisation and health difficulties are very common, underpinned by a range of complex biological mechanisms, as well as distorted thinking, learned behaviours (e.g., throwing oneself into work and ignoring bodily needs for rest and exercise), and compounded behaviour patterns. Overall, the traumatised world often feels overwhelming. There is little certainty and no apparent structure; people remain unsafe, relationships are confusing, and above all, many trauma survivors trust *no one*, least of all themselves.

The traumatised mind: trauma changes how we think

All human beings are born with a special ability and a part of the brain that sets us apart from other animals. This part of the brain is the prefrontal cortex and it's very well developed in humans, giving us the ability to engage in complex thought, including thinking about the past and future, planning, organising, and making complex decisions. These are some of the simpler cognitive functions we possess; however, the same abilities that confer on us these great advantages can also cause great difficulties (e.g., worrying about whether we will lose our jobs, ruminating about a partner leaving us). Many of our thoughts are based on habitual thinking patterns, or heuristics (cognitive shortcuts we take to simplify information processing, such as 'dark alleyways are dangerous'), and this can lead to significant difficulties for trauma survivors whose thinking habits are often unconsciously based on traumatic events.

From a neurobiological standpoint, the traumatised brain[1] is unique. It has difficulty understanding and organising threats, is hyper-fixated on noticing danger (with correspondingly reduced capacities to pay attention to other sensory inputs and developmental tasks), struggles with modulating emotionally arousing sensory inputs, and has trouble with forming memories. Attention and concentration are likely to be affected, as are executive functioning capacities (e.g., thinking, planning, and delaying gratification). Certain trauma survivors may have been exposed to substances in the womb or have acquired brain injuries, and then all of these difficulties are compounded. The chronically traumatised body struggles to regulate physiological arousal levels (i.e., constantly remaining in danger mode) with high levels of stress hormones and associated problems with biological processes such as heart rate and blood pressure. Fundamentally, the body and brain work in tandem, and survivors of complex traumas typically have a high physiological load to carry, and a number of psychological difficulties with deep roots in the biological processes that occur during traumas.

When we consider thoughts, we are really thinking of neural patterns or activity in the brain. Thoughts have two elements: the content and the form. The *content* refers to *what* we think about (e.g., what happened at work today), and the *form* refers to *how* we think about it (e.g., ruminating about issues, expecting the worst, filtering out the positive, jumping to conclusions, or being very black and white or rigid in our thinking). Both can be problematic on occasion, but especially so when put together. It's common for threat-attuned trauma survivors to develop thinking patterns based on identifying danger and responding to loss and rejection. Over time, these patterns become characterological, much like the defence mechanisms we noted earlier. It can be helpful to understand these patterns, as there is a close nexus between emotions, thoughts, and behaviours, and all of these come together to create mental health difficulties.

Some of these patterns include:

Catastrophising

The trauma victim often anticipates the worst and focuses on that outcome, ignoring other, more positive possibilities. The key here is anticipating that disaster will strike and allowing thoughts to fall down a dark spiral, magnifying both the extent of the potential disaster as well as the likelihood that it will occur. Here is an example of this kind of thinking: 'I wonder why my boss has asked me for a meeting this afternoon. I wonder if she thinks I am doing a bad job. Maybe I will get fired. I won't be able to pay my mortgage if this happens. What happens if I become homeless?' Trauma survivors are very attuned to what can go wrong.

Black and white thinking

Black and white thinking is focused on extremes. Things are all or nothing; people are either all good or all bad. There are no shades of grey in this thinking style. Examples include, 'If he is angry, he is dangerous', 'If I don't succeed at first try, I must be a failure', or 'All men are bad'. Binaries like these can feel protective, defending victims against harm. If people and situations can be quickly and neatly categorised, then the victim can avoid potentially harmful situations.

Black and white thinking extends well beyond the ambit of the trauma victim — it's deeply embedded in society today, as we access more information and become more certain of our views and wholly intolerant of views that run counter to our own.

Shoulds

We all have certain guidelines that we use to map our course in life. These can become problematic when they morph into rigid rules or 'shoulds', with no space for movement; this can happen when relational trauma has involved tight control over a victim or unachievably high standards of behaviour. These 'shoulds' can be directed towards ourselves ('I should always be in control', 'I should always have the house clean') or other people ('My friends should always be there to support me', 'My partner should always answer the phone when I call').

Emotional reasoning

Emotional reasoning means experiencing a feeling and then reasoning based on that (e.g., 'I feel anxious and therefore this situation must be dangerous'). As may be expected, trauma survivors experience high levels of anxiety, shame, hopelessness, and sadness. Sometimes, these emotional experiences can colour how they see the world. It is helpful to remember that feelings can also sometimes just be habits, rather than reflecting reality, and that feelings can influence how we think, and vice versa.

Filtering

This is a very common thinking style, and it's actually quite helpful from an evolutionary perspective. It involves filtering out all the positive and focusing exclusively on the negative. It may be amplified after trauma, because trauma involves something threatening. This is adaptive, because human brains are attuned to look for danger to keep us alive and safe, but an overemphasis on the negative can detract from our ability to notice the positive and to experience hope, happiness, or joy.

Jumping to conclusions

This involves the belief that one knows what will occur or what someone is thinking or feeling without stopping to check the facts or considering alternative explanations. An example might be, 'My friend has ignored my call — they must be angry with me, and not want to be my friend anymore.' This is a very common thinking style for the threat-attuned traumatised mind, so keenly alert to any interpersonal threat and loss.

Anna and I looked at these patterns together and found that she struggled with all of them at various times. This is very common for complex trauma survivors. She catastrophised frequently and assumed that the worst would happen — leaving her stuck in huge anxiety spirals. She also held extremely high standards for herself and punished herself by cutting when she 'failed' (her word, not mine). She made decisions based purely on how she felt about something (e.g., feeling distant from a partner and ending a relationship without any further appraisal). This emotional reasoning had led to great isolation. Our work involved drawing attention to these patterns as they arose and building more flexible ways of thinking.

Behavioural patterns

In addition to difficulties with forms and habits of thinking (i.e., *how* one thinks), survivors often have a range of beliefs about the world and themselves (i.e., *what* one thinks) and these beliefs are commonly expressed in a range of moment-to-moment behaviours across relationships, work, and self-regard. What people do is intimately linked with how they think and what they feel — and most behaviours (even seeming 'accidents') hold deep meaning about how a person perceives and responds to the world. There are few behaviours that are true accidents, and reflecting on the function of a behaviour (i.e., what it is trying to communicate) and its motivations is a key part of therapy. External chaos often mirrors internal chaos,[2] and some typical trauma-driven patterns include self-sabotaging behaviours and the repetition compulsion (i.e., making choices that seem to inadvertently repeat the initial trauma). It can be helpful to understand some of these patterns when considering the impacts of relational trauma.

Self-sabotaging

At its most basic, self-sabotage involves undermining one's own goals, desires, or successes. It includes a range of behaviours, such as difficulty committing to goals, identifying goals so lofty that we are sure to fail (which sets up a feedback loop of negative emotion and low self-efficacy), not planning or problem-solving appropriately, engaging in self-defeating actions that go against a goal we have set, not fully committing to a goal or plan, or pre-emptively withdrawing and shying away from a success. When thinking of Anna, her behaviour at the end of therapy (i.e., disappearing without a goodbye, and with a fee outstanding) could be seen as an act of self-sabotage. It helped her close the door: 'Ahona is probably angry with me and I can't go back'. She had engaged in similar acts in her other relationships, ruefully confessing that a part of her wanted closeness (and psychological change), while another part of her preferred things to stay as they were.

While most of us self-sabotage at various times in a range of ways (e.g., planning to go to the gym and then refusing to get out of bed on time), this appears an especially common pattern with some complex trauma survivors, who may have particular difficulties with learned helplessness, low self-esteem or self-efficacy, and planning and modulating realistic action. Self-efficacy is our confidence in our capacity to manage a certain situation or to effect change in our lives. It is probably one of the most vital psychological competencies we can build, because it lies at the heart of our belief that we can change our lives, learn new things, or develop better behaviours and patterns. With low self-efficacy, we're likely to experience learned helplessness and not even *contemplate* making changes, because we don't believe that we will succeed.

Difficulties with managing emotion can underpin this: intolerance of discomfort, deep fear of success and change, and a reluctance to upset the safety of the proverbial apple cart. There are also a variety of gains involved with seemingly self-sabotaging behaviours. For example, expressing anger in violent ways might bring about negative consequences, but it can also allow a person to gain status from peers, to avoid something aversive, or to reinforce their sense of themselves as someone who *can* effect change in their world, (when their typical lives may offer them few opportunities to demonstrate this).

For some survivors, the abuse occurred concurrently with other incredibly difficult circumstances (such as parental incarceration or substance abuse) rendering life chaotic and complex. Self-sabotaging behaviours may not be sabotage as much as an inability to relate to the world in any other way. The term 'sabotage' implies a level of choice, but it's important to ensure that we don't attribute choice where there was none.

The repetition compulsion

This is probably one of the most harmful post-traumatic patterns I've worked with. It's not very well understood, and there are a lot of myths about why survivors find themselves in situations that closely mirror an initial trauma. Each time a traumatic event recurs, it strengthens the initial patterns of response and creates new ones, amplifying a survivor's difficulties. When looking at the repetition compulsion, most people (professionals and laypeople alike) tend to blame the victim for their poor choices. Sometimes people instead adopt a 'poor them' attitude and discount any agency that victims have, or become furious and call it 'victim-blaming' when people are encouraged to think about the way their choices might have contributed to traumatic experiences. Unfortunately, choosing not to see these things out of fear of hurt feelings or offence might mean that patterns are never changed. It is important for compassion to be balanced with a drive to change and heal, and this can only come with clear sight. To manage this, I try to find a balance: understanding the patterns that might lead to the repetition compulsion, while remaining non-judgemental and compassionate.

The repetition compulsion can manifest in a range of ways, often within relationships. People will find that they enter intimate relationships that mirror early difficult relationships, either with a parent or partner. This was Anna's pattern, and she spoke about the way most of her partners were cold and withdrawn like her mother, often leaving her chasing love. Sometimes, it plays out in the areas of work, where people experience bullying, or with friends and family. Sometimes, the revictimisation can take the form of a chaotic lifestyle, including a snowball effect of problems with relationships, work, employment, and housing — with each contributing to the next.

I have intimate knowledge of this pattern myself. Within my early life and childhood, I experienced a range of difficulties that left me feeling isolated and defective. I entered adolescence with a deep need to belong, and a deep sense of shame about who I was. I had been conditioned to accept a range of abusive behaviours and to inhabit a caretaking role, at huge cost to myself. My radar for abuse was non-existent and in my attempt to find belonging, I entered a complex and difficult relationship, and spent some time in a group characterised by religious control and abuse.

At the end of the relationship, to manage my low mood, anxiety, and trauma history, I started seeing a psychologist. I desperately needed care and a firm attachment. The psychologist I chose was confident and authoritative, but over time it became clear that she had some beliefs that troubled me. In our first session, she asked me whether my parents were involved in Eastern religion. 'Yeah, they are Hindu', I said, not knowing then that this was an unusual intake-session question. She started speaking about matters such as demonic possession and deliverance (i.e., the belief that demons can cause mental illness and need to be exorcised from people). She gave me information about things like 'soul ties' and 'demonic entry points' through activities such as yoga, Eastern religion, and sex outside marriage, and often reiterated that there was no healing without Jesus. She said that most trauma survivors could only 'limp along' until they engaged in work involving things like breaking 'ungodly soul ties', asking Jesus to 'take away parts', and casting out demons; and she once invited me to her church to hear someone talk about this type of 'healing'. I was terrified and felt that I would need to change my agnostic spiritual orientation to engage in this form of therapy or I would continue to struggle. I tried the Christianity hat on for a while, but it never sat right for me — especially not this set of beliefs. And of course, this felt like my earlier experiences of religious abuse, though I had entered therapy to escape and heal them, not to *repeat* them.

I was in great pain, and very confused and alone. I didn't tell anyone about what was happening in my therapy until I left. While it may be easy to ask why I didn't tell someone, or just stop going, the answers were complex and centred around attachment. I knew that if I told anyone, it would force me to confront what was happening. Ignoring it was easier.

It took me two years to end this therapy, and when I did, I was left in a shambolic psychological state. The problems for which I had initially sought therapy had remained largely untreated and were now compounded by a new attachment trauma and the fear this therapy had stirred up in me. It was hard for me to understand the connection between my earlier traumas and my new difficulty, and even harder for me to try to separate from this psychologist and take action against her. Although she had cared for me at a time I needed care and *had* provided some basic help with my mood, she had also breached boundaries.

Such is the paradox of relational trauma.

With the wisdom of hindsight, I can see how attempting to satisfy deep, unmet needs and a lack of boundaries or a radar for the psychologically unsafe led me into such situations. None of them were my fault — I couldn't have been expected to protect myself from that which I could not see (and I should certainly not have had to protect myself from a health practitioner) — but part of my recovery involved understanding this pattern and working hard to change it (by creating better boundaries and becoming more aware of my own psychological patterns).

My next psychologist (who I still see to this day, almost 13 years later) is self-effacing and gentle. I was a little unsure after our first session, but it also felt important to move away from my pattern of picking confident people who seemed to promise that they could 'fix' me. She didn't promise me anything, but she was patient and kind and sat with me in all my distress, and the confusing story I brought to her. (She also told me she wasn't Christian, which helped.) It took me years to trust her properly. The work for the first few years was really about working through what had happened with my former psychologist, and learning to trust that I would not be betrayed in a similar way.

People fall into the repetition compulsion for various reasons: as a way of fulfilling unmet needs; through a lack of good boundaries; by not understanding signs that signal harmful behaviours; and by being instinctively drawn to behaviours and personalities that are known and familiar — even though familiar can also mean harmful. Deeply held beliefs about one's worth (e.g., 'I don't deserve any better') are also at play, as is the social context of our lives (e.g., the industry we work in, our partner) — if we're surrounded by people who use substances and engage in crime, we're more likely to find ourselves in situations where we are victimised. At other times, we're unconsciously drawn to dynamics resembling the abuses we have suffered as a means of trying to achieve a better ending for ourselves — we continue to enact the trauma until we are able to flip the script, change our ways of responding to people who harm, and find the way to a new interpersonal paradigm.

Interestingly, I found that once I had taken concrete steps to confront my former psychologist, and report her to the regulatory bodies, I could see and address other challenging relationships in my life — I was no longer drawn to people who harmed me. I developed a far better radar for these behaviours, and felt more empowered, which led to greater trust in my own ability to protect myself from harm.

I will undoubtedly continue to meet difficult people and encounter harmful situations, but re-enacting the early harms I suffered, and being able to rewrite an ending for myself, in conjunction with excellent therapy, have been strong enough to change my habitual responses to people who hold power.

The terror of emotions

An emotion is a feeling that arises from one's internal processes, relationship with others, or current situation. All emotions have neurobiological markers (i.e., distinct changes in the body and brain as an emotion is experienced) and involve bodily changes and cues; common ones include anger, sadness, fear, disgust, love, shock, joy, shame, happiness, and guilt.

All emotions have a function, or purpose. They are evolutionarily designed to provide signals and help us stay alive. For instance, disgust is likely to give us a clue that something is rotten or likely to make us unwell, whereas love will help us pair bond, ensuring the continuity of the species.

As our world has increased in complexity, emotions too have morphed, generalised, and taken on new functions and meanings. It's no longer sabre-toothed tigers that cause anxiety and fear; instead, we fear more amorphous things, like loss, rejection, or public speaking. To understand feelings, it can be helpful to consider their function: a feeling of sadness might keep us cocooned at home, giving us the quiet time we need to process a loss. It may also be designed to communicate to other people that we need support. Anger can protect us and may also act as a signal to people to give us some space.

Emotions are not problematic in and of themselves. I often wrestle with this concept in my work, as people come in with the idea that certain emotions are problematic (e.g., anger) — usually because they weren't encouraged within the family home or broader culture. All emotions are designed for a reason, though, and we all have our own emotional map, formed by what was encouraged in our families and by our own temperaments. Emotions can become problematic because of how we express them (i.e., being angry is okay, hitting someone else is not), when they are too intense, or when they change too frequently.

One of the major difficulties trauma clients encounter lies in how they experience, understand, and express feelings. At its most basic, relational trauma is a psychological injury that elicits deep feelings of anger, sadness, and fear. If we have good emotional processing, we experience feelings and are able to acknowledge them (even if just to ourselves), are supported through them, understand why they are arising, and use them as information to decide how to proceed (e.g., if angry, perhaps we need to consider whether someone is hurting us). With relational trauma, this normal processing is thwarted almost immediately — it is often impossible to fully acknowledge the trauma and the overwhelming emotions that arise, and to feel angry about it, within the relationship where the trauma occurred. One can allow the feelings *or* keep the relationship. Often, the emotions themselves are overpowering, and survivors may not have had the capacity to build any emotional management skills.

Typically, survivors push their traumas away or pretend that they weren't so bad, invalidating their own experiences. They are likely to also be invalidated by the perpetrator (and other people invested in maintaining the status quo), being told 'Don't cry', or 'There's no need to be angry', or 'You're overreacting' (how I dislike this word! I make it a point in my practice to only use 'strong reaction'). They may have received specific and subtle training in reducing and denying their own emotional responses, to best serve the interests of the perpetrator ('Stop crying, it wasn't so bad').

Sometimes, when difficult emotion is denied or repressed, it can express itself in startling and explosive ways, including:

- Difficulties with numbness — some clients desperately want to feel something but report that they cannot, while others will suddenly shut down during a fight or when a relationship is becoming more intense. I've had clients who report that they 'fall out of love' when a partner seeks some commitment or clarity; this sudden emotional numbing sometimes reflects avoidant attachment patterns and trauma-driven detachment from intimacy.

- Emotions that change rapidly, sometimes from minute to minute.
- Emotions that are very strong for the context, such as feeling betrayed and completely abandoned because a friend says they can't see us.
- A general sense of free-floating rage and hatred directed at the world and other people, instead of specific anger directed at a perpetrator. I often see survivors who appear to be angry at everything, which often means they have not processed their anger towards the people who hurt them. Anger that is not directed at a specific source, and which is based on unrealistic expectations, is generally anger that can't be processed — often hurting only the person experiencing it.
- Deep unhappiness and a sense that one does not belong anywhere.
- Strong sensitivity to rejection.
- Apathy, low mood, and helplessness.
- Extreme anxiety and worry about what might happen.

Difficulties with intense emotion are the reason many trauma survivors use substances (such as alcohol or illicit substances). Many substances have affective-dampening effects, essentially helping numb emotions that feel too strong. Other substances (such as methamphetamine) confer an illusory sense of confidence and happiness, which can be highly tempting for those who usually have a bleak or difficult emotional landscape. Substance use can be very problematic for the trauma survivor. It often becomes the only way someone knows to cope, and most substances have huge long-term impacts on mental health and physical health, despite the short-term solace they offer. For other people, substance use can lead into cycles of engaging in offending behaviour, and lifestyle chaos. Usually, when working with survivors, I focus on reducing reliance on substances and developing more adaptive coping skills. This doesn't always mean complete abstinence (though there are some very harmful substances I strongly encourage full abstinence from, like methamphetamine) but at least a significant reduction in use and ensuring that substances are used recreationally, rather than to manage life. For some survivors who have had serious problems with substance use, abstinence is a must.

While most jurisdictions in Australia criminalise substance use (except alcohol), this is not aligned with the pragmatics of work in the health field. I largely see substance use as a health issue, not a criminal justice issue, and remind my clients that I am not the police when they sidle around discussing their weekend MDMA or cannabis use with me (though I may then make them explore in excruciating detail what led to the use, as well as why they didn't try other mechanisms of mood management first).

Relational trauma within intimate relationships in adulthood can also cause significant trouble with managing emotion. Intimate relationships very closely mirror the attachment relationships we have/had with our parents and can quickly aggravate existing wounds or create wounds where there were none. I've had a range of clients who have experienced intimate partner violence and without fail, all of them recollect being more scared of the perpetrators than they thought possible and being horrified at the strength of their sadness and fear in the relationship, or their anguish when it ended. Intimate partner violence and coercive control are so challenging psychologically *because* of the damage they cause, or re-activate, within our attachment and emotional management systems.

What is emotional regulation or management?

Emotional regulation or management involves recognising when emotions are arising, understanding them, and responding to them in a flexible and context-dependent manner (i.e., how one expresses sadness at work can be very different to how one would express it to a partner). It does not involve shutting feelings down, or conversely, fully indulging and expressing every single feeling that might arise. Emotions are information — *not* fact — and good emotional management means using them pragmatically, while allowing regular flow.

We initially learn to soothe and manage emotion from our caregivers — this is the bedrock of how we develop regulation skills. Over time, we watch our parents and other people around us, and learn how to manage feelings through the modelling we receive from them. Families typically have characteristic emotional habitats, including emotions that are discouraged, ways of expressing emotion that are accepted, and the reactions people have.

Emotional regulation learning can be interrupted in many ways.

- Caregivers struggle to reliably soothe a baby when it is distressed, leading to dysregulation, at the pre-verbal stage, in emotional management. These children learn to self-soothe by detaching from scary emotional experiences and entering a state of learned helplessness, since they know help will not be forthcoming.
- Caregivers who have limited emotional management capacities themselves and model unhelpful behaviours, such as shutting down when sad, drinking alcohol to numb, reacting with violence when angry, or providing damaging messages, such as 'boys don't cry'.
- Social influences, including from teachers, peers, and the media. I remember talking to a client I was seeing for policing-related PTSD and asking her where she

believed her initial difficulties with blocking out emotion came from. 'Chuck Norris,' she said, matter-of-factly. 'I was raised on a diet of Chuck Norris, John Wayne, Bruce Lee, and Clint Eastwood.' This gave rise to a strong sense of stoicism, which meant she didn't seek support when she was assaulted at work.

- An early life characterised by intense circumstances or chaos (e.g., a very sick sibling, parental substance use) that meant adequate attention could not be paid to helping a child develop self-soothing skills. This may also have caused more distress than a child's developing nervous system could tolerate.

These factors often work in tandem; people struggle to manage emotion and may get in trouble for this (e.g., fights at school, difficulties keeping friends, or isolation), which can mean either that they have few relationships or develop problematic relationships that evoke and reinforce already felt distress. Much of good emotional regulation is the fit between a person's environment and their needs, and it is almost impossible to form good, healthy emotional management when one's environment is abusive, threatening, invalidating, or dismissive.

Anna had many of the difficulties with emotion common in other survivors. She almost always repressed emotion and found herself feeling 'numb'. Occasionally, emotion burst out of her in an uncontrollable way, sending her fleeing into shame and self-harm as a way of punishing herself. Learning to simply recognise and name the emotions she felt was a big task and involved much work with the part of her that preferred to feel detached and found safety in numbness.

Trauma and fractured relationships

It is within human relationships that people both experience relational trauma and can heal from it. This paradox is what causes terror for survivors and can sometimes lead to feedback loops of bad relationships → unmet needs → frantic attempts to form relationships to meet those needs → bad relationships → compounded trauma.

When considering trauma, relationships and attachment play a central role. Abusive or difficult relationships can short-circuit our ability to attach, to recognise the characteristics of healthy and unhealthy relationships, to understand boundaries, and to use relationships and co-regulation (i.e., managing emotion by attuning to another person's calming signals) as healing mechanisms. We must understand, recognise, and build good relationships, to ensure that we don't inadvertently revictimise ourselves by forming close relationships with unsafe people. We are social beings, and we need a range of safe connections in our life.

Understanding trauma attachment impacts

Attachment[3] is the biological drive to connect with other people. Human babies are helpless for the first few years of their lives and need to attach to caregivers to survive. This drive is hard-wired into us. We all have an attachment style[4] that we build through our initial relationships with caregivers. These styles permeate everything we do and all our deeper relationships. They mostly play out in the arena of intimate relationships but can emerge in friendships and other relationships, too. Fundamentally, attachment patterns involve two dynamics: the push and the pull. The push is a drive for independence and autonomy, as seen when a baby ventures forth from its mother's arms to seek the new. The pull is a pull towards someone else, for closeness, care, and intimacy. Attachment requires a balance between the two, because we need both independence and closeness. Attachment wounds (caused by caregivers who were punishing, inconsistent, or unreliable) lead to issues with closeness, including people who experience anxiety about being close to people and those who experience anxiety without close relationships.

The heart of attachment: finding a secure base

At the heart of attachment theory is the 'secure base': the relationship/s that we return to over and over, as a means of seeking connection and safety before we venture forth again. We all need a secure base, ideally a few, and our key relationships should provide it. Our first secure bases likely took the form of caregivers. When we're adults, our secure bases reside in intimate partners and other key figures, such as therapists and friends. We use these bases in similar ways, returning to them for debriefing, comfort, and care before heading back out into the world. With relational trauma, however, this process may have been disrupted — especially if initial abuse was perpetrated by caregivers — or if later secure bases have proven unstable (even if the earliest bases gave us a good start).

Attachment Styles
- Secure ('I'm okay and you are okay'): Secure adults are those raised by caregivers who were available, soothing, nurturing, and not overly punitive. Securely attached adults are comfortable with closeness, able to be autonomous, can commit to relationships, pace contact and disclosure, are not too quick to perceive rejection, are able to soothe themselves, and soothe other people. Securely attached individuals will likely be able to assess

and evaluate people to determine if relationships feel right, will be okay being alone but also value relationships. They will be able to manage their own emotions and will be open and sharing in relationships and friendships. They are likely to be responsive, have healthy boundaries, not try to form relationships too quickly, and not be overly jealous or demanding.

- Anxious ('I really need you. Don't leave me'): Anxious attachments are often created by caregivers who were neglectful or unavailable, resulting in a deep need for closeness and a fear of being left alone. Other forms of abuse can also lead to this attachment style. Anxiously attached people will often develop intense feelings quickly, struggle to be independent, and may exhibit strong attachment bids (e.g., needing frequent contact). They may feel they never receive enough closeness and may violate boundaries and push people away with their need for support and reassurance. They are quick to perceive rejection, and may form intense and premature connections (think: being sure one has met the love of one's life, or best friend, after just one meeting), may attempt to make constant contact, become agitated or demanding without frequent contact (e.g., 'are you upset with me, why haven't you responded?'), attempt to hasten the pace of new connections (e.g., seeing someone every night for a week), disclose too much too quickly, exhibit jealousy, or otherwise try to make a relationship develop more quickly than it should. Attempting to form attachments too quickly often short-circuits the process of getting to know someone, making it harder to assess their personality and true motivation. As a result, people with anxious attachment styles may form a close relationship with someone harmful or remain in a harmful relationship.

- Avoidant ('I don't need you'): Avoidant attachments often stem from caregivers who were inconsistent, rejecting, or unresponsive, forcing people to depend only on themselves. Avoidant adults struggle with reliance and may be hyper-independent, have difficulty with being close to people, and withdraw or reject people when distressed. Their close friends/partners/family may not feel heard or seen or may feel disposable. Avoidant adults often prefer freedom and independence, and their troubles with committing to close relationships are born out of a desire to maintain this freedom. People with avoidant traits may appear confusing in all manner of close relationships — they may withdraw after a period of closeness, hold their cards close to their chest, be unable or unwilling to allow a relationship to become deeper, prefer to keep things quite impersonal or casual, never form close relationships, describe themselves as 'loners', pull away just as the connection is starting to feel stronger, and not want to talk about key areas of life. This attachment pattern often separates people from the social connections we all need, reducing the supports they can access when things get difficult.

- Fearful-Avoidant ('I don't need you, go away. NO, come back', also called disorganised attachment): The classic push-pull dynamic. This attachment dynamic often develops when caregivers are abusive and it manifests as being uncomfortable about closeness — and thus withdrawing or rejecting a partner — but then worrying about not having enough commitment or closeness and attempting to seek connection. This dynamic can be especially confusing for people unless they are able to see the attachment patterns at play. Fearful-avoidant behaviours serve to keep people at arm's length, stopping the person from accessing truly close, consistent, and stable relationships. Other people might respond initially by drawing closer, then becoming confused by inconsistency, and pulling away, thus cementing the initial attachment style. When people speak of trauma bonding, they often refer to a disorganised or fearful-avoidant attachment style, and the impact this can have on intimate relationships, especially when both partners have attachment difficulties.

While I have presented these attachment styles as discrete, we often oscillate between them and demonstrate traits from each. They're not fixed entities but rather *tendencies*. We can be securely attached in one relationship, and more anxious in another. We form attachment patterns within relationships in tandem with the others involved. Overall, though, trauma is characterised by a lack of safety in relationships, regardless of which attachment style we tend towards.

To process and heal from trauma, safe attachments are vital, and understanding our attachment patterns is the first step. Changing them is a slow process but is entirely possible. It requires the careful selection of safe people and behaviour that isn't aligned with our instinctive patterns, allowing our brains to lay down new neural pathways that will help form new patterns. Working on attachment lets us build relationships that are more likely to meet our core psychological needs, which can aid in healing. Ideally, survivors will learn to slowly move towards a state of secure attachments, where the tension between closeness and independence can be maintained.

Therapy is a powerful tool for this: it allows careful and safe attachment, where the survivor can experience having some of their needs met, and may feel truly *seen*, perhaps for the first time in their lives. Forming close and steady relationships can be healing at several levels. First, they allow survivors to access supports when needed. While calling on a friend to bring us groceries when we are sick can seem like a small thing, it can mean the difference between feeling supported and cared for or feeling completely alone. Good, consistent relationships allow us to build a steady bedrock of support that means we have access to people we can ask for care and advice.

My work with Anna also involved exploring her attachment patterns in detail and helping her understand why she was often drawn to avoidant partners. It is common for people to select partners with attachment styles that evoke early wounding (e.g., someone with an anxious attachment style may select an avoidant partner who resembles a rejecting parent), and awareness of this pattern is key. Anna and I also worked on encouraging emotional expression and co-regulating with her in therapy while encouraging her to use relationships and attachments outside therapy to soothe. Ideally, she would have learnt to accept that she did need people and would have shifted some of the shame she felt, though she ended therapy before this could happen.

Key ways of relating after trauma

I have noticed that people develop a number of characteristic patterns of relating after experiences of abuse in relationships. Some of these are direct consequences of abuse, while others develop as compensations for the way the abuse changed someone's view of the world. There are many reasons people engage in some of these behavioural patterns, and not all these reasons are trauma based.

People-pleasing (sometimes called fawning)

Many survivors spend time with people who have eroded their sense of self and/or blamed them for things that happened. They may have developed an internalised sense of 'badness' or shame and will try to compensate for this by being 'good' and pleasing people out of fear. Fear of key figures in one's life or being conditioned to put one's needs last can also result in this behaviour, as the survivor desperately attempts to placate people.

Over time, this behaviour can become a way of being and generalise to all relationships. I have worked with survivors who don't realise that this is their default, and it is only when I point out behaviours that suggest they are inhabiting the 'good client' role (e.g., always agreeing with me) that they start to consider it. This pattern can be highly detrimental, as it stops people from establishing real relationships based on mutual support and meeting needs. At a more malignant level, it may mean that the survivor is so focused on pleasing people that they do not identify difficult relationships until immersed in them, setting up cycles of revictimisation. If we are always focused on pleasing someone, we don't give ourselves the time to stop and consider whether we actually like or trust them.

Enmeshment — or losing oneself in a relationship completely

This is similar to the anxious attachment patterns described earlier, but it goes a step further, into a total loss of identity and independence within relationships, including a complete lack of boundaries. Enmeshment can occur when boundaries have not been accepted, encouraged, or modelled, or when someone has experienced a smothering relationship with no boundaries. It's often seen with 'parentification', as this involves a complete breach of the structural boundaries that should exist in healthy and functional families. Parentified children learn to abandon their developing identities to merge with their parents, and they carry this pattern into other relationships.

Enmeshment can include not fully understanding what one likes or desires as distinct from another person, being unable to tolerate someone else having difficulties or feelings and needing to swoop in and rescue, being unable to make decisions without seeking feedback from someone else, and being unable to tolerate separation. Sometimes when people use the word 'empath' as shorthand for strongly experiencing other people's feelings, they are referring to their tendency to form enmeshed relationships without boundaries or a separation between one's feelings and another person's. Empathy is powerful and is good, but if it runs unchecked and is so strong that we become swamped, then we can't really engage well with the world.

Hyper-independence

This involves being so self-reliant that one is unable to allow or seek any help or support from other people. This often develops as a compensatory mechanism after abuse or neglect (i.e., 'no one is going to be there anyway/people are always going to hurt me, so why bother?'). This pattern can also develop when children are punished for being 'needy' by caregivers who pathologise the very normal needs and emotions of a young child.

It is not possible for anyone to exist in a complete social vacuum so people with this pattern often attempt to make connections despite their deep reserve, but are either unable to fully commit to connections or cannot allow people to become close, thereby fulfilling their initial predictions that people are unsafe, and reinforcing the pattern. This pattern is common with avoidant attachment styles.

Martyred victimhood

People who have experienced abuse *are* victims, but occasionally, people develop a sense of identity centred wholly around being traumatised. They fail to recognise the agency they have in other situations in life and adopt a state of learned helplessness, which reinforces both the original trauma and their perception of themself as a victim. It's common for people to develop a victim mode as a defence against the world — after all, if we present ourselves as vulnerable and in need of care, people will provide that care. This way of being can occur when the initial abuse involves power and control, so that the survivor feels they have no agency and there is no point trying to develop any. This pattern can also develop as a form of detached and passive-aggressive communication. If you're the victim, then other people need to subjugate their own needs to soothe you; this can provide many secondary gains (e.g., having a partner always give in to what you want because you start crying during arguments and say that they are triggering memories of your bad childhood).

Sometimes, martyred victims stay in harmful relationships or accept negative behaviours because they don't believe they can change situations for themselves, and may enter cycles of repeated revictimisation. Sometimes, they feel a strong sense of moral righteousness and build compensatory entitlement ('I am entitled to do what I say and want, because people have wronged me and the world now needs to make up for it'), falling into exhibiting interpersonally harmful behaviours themselves.

This trait can arise when there are problematic personality features accompanying a trauma history, such as strong borderline, narcissistic, or dependent traits. It's common to see this in certain sections of the forensic population, too: for example, 'I only hurt people because I was hurt first, and I have no control over it.'

4

The Tasks of Relational Trauma Recovery

In this chapter, we'll explore the main tasks of healing from relational trauma, and discuss the treatment landscape, including suitable therapies and the key qualities needed from therapists. There are many misconceptions about treatment held by survivors and therapists alike, and both parties may feel overwhelmed by the range of issues that survivors can present with.

Trauma work can feel overwhelming when there are many difficulties and diagnoses, and it can, at first, consist mainly of putting out psychic spot fires (i.e., managing crises in daily life). For many survivors, the work never progresses beyond this stage, and people can spend years in therapy talking about the minutiae of daily living — fights with friends, difficulties with relationships, substance use, trouble with jobs — without ever engaging in the guts of trauma work. It can feel as if therapy is stalling when stuck in this pattern — and is especially common when a non trauma–trained therapist is working with a survivor and the relationship between the abuse and the difficulties that have brought someone to therapy have not been explored. It's essential to hold the larger tasks of recovery in mind, and to consider how the smaller 'spot fires' are related to the bigger blaze of trauma, as well as to openly discuss this pattern once it is noticed.

Not everything I discuss below is applicable to all survivors. Some of my clients have very safe lives and relationships when they come to me, and we don't need to do much work there. Instead, we might focus on understanding their trauma-driven patterns of responding, to see, for example, why they find it so hard to stand up to toxic members of their family. This list is not linear, and it's not a checklist. People will usually work on a few of these tasks at the same time in therapy, and will move back and forth between them. There is no specific order to follow, beyond noting that *acknowledging* the trauma is often one of the first steps. Even this can feel terrifying for some survivors, and therapists must tread carefully.

Healing will look different for each survivor. There is no imperative to thrive (though I do wish this for everyone who has been hurt), no certain pathway one must take, and no therapy one *must* engage in for healing. No survivor has to speak out against a perpetrator or fight for justice. Sometimes, just the quietness of being is enough. Ultimately, the work for each survivor will look a little different and life post-recovery will also look different. For some people, it will look like speaking up and using their pain in service of change; others may want to move on completely; and for yet others simply existing with some calm will be enough. These are equally valid paths.

Healing from interpersonal traumas can require a suite of supports and different tasks. It can be a lengthy process and can require that life continues to be lived in the cracks meanwhile. It is in the minutiae of living well — regulating one's mood, finding one's unique meaning, acceptance that perhaps just being is enough, glimpses of happiness, kindness, stability in work, safety in friends and close others, moments of laughter and connection — that survivors will often find the ballast needed to launch themselves forward.

Sometimes healing is active, but at other times it is in the fallow spaces between engaging in psychological work that we can find some true growth. Ultimately, finding a meaning for life bigger than the trauma helps, though I acknowledge the enormity of this task for those who have suffered huge harms at an early age.

Naming and accepting the traumas

It is important to acknowledge what one has experienced, and that events were abusive or traumatic, instead of sheltering behind dissociation and denial. Survivors find it very hard to accept what happened to them, and a big part of working with them will involve unpicking thoughts such as: 'If I had fought back' (this wouldn't have happened …); 'If I had not allowed him into my room' (this wouldn't have happened …); 'If I had told someone sooner' (this wouldn't have happened …). The subtext is rarely articulated, but it's the basis of many survivors' roadblocks to recovery. Using hindsight bias and believing that something may not have happened if we had just done X or Y can be protection against having to accept that awful things happen sometimes, but it can also create guilt and shame in victims. Hindsight bias is a form of cognitive bias. Once a situation has occurred, hindsight bias can make that event seem more predictable than it actually was. Basically, traumas can happen at any time, and bad things can happen to good people — but they won't happen all the time, and threat perception needs to be carefully managed.

There is usually little we can do to control the original occurrence of a trauma, because inflicting it is largely about the perpetrator's behaviour and choices, not the victim's choices.

Accepting the trauma does not mean allowing it or believing it was okay, but it's an important part of recovery — the past cannot be changed, and moving forward requires some acceptance that the harms occurred so we can process them. 'Radical acceptance' is useful, and is a term derived from dialectical behaviour therapy. It means accepting what happened and what is — though not approving of it.

Processing trauma memories

Regardless of the nature of the harm, it's likely that the survivor will have some incredibly difficult memories about it. With complex relational traumas or events that occur at an early age, it may be hard to pinpoint specific events or to recall full details. This may also be the case with standalone events, such as a sexual assault, because when under severe stress the brain processes information differently and can change how memories are formed. Some of the ways in which my clients have described their memories, include:

'I only remember her voice.'

'I remember the feel of the belt and crying — but I can't remember what I did to make him hit me.'

'Every time I see the colour blue, I remember the shirt he was wearing.'

'I can't stand to think about it; every time I remember it, I drink.'

'A black hole … sudden flashes and I can't control when they come up.'

Some memories can be crystal clear and recur frequently and uncontrollably. They can also feel very fragmented and perhaps focus on only one aspect or part of the experience. There may be no narrative consistency. They may be highly painful or have no emotion at all associated with them. We may remember more memories with time. We may be unsure whether we are imagining that something occurred or remembering that it did occur. All of this is normal.

There are different schools of thought on whether survivors need to discuss and explore their memories. I've had great results using cognitive processing therapy with victims, without focusing too much on the memories. Other modalities — such as eye movement desensitisation and reprocessing (EMDR) and prolonged exposure (I speak about all these in more detail later in the chapter) — rely on engaging in exposure and effectively rewiring the brain's way of holding and presenting trauma memories. I usually let the victim lead. Many people find it incredibly helpful to be witnessed as they talk about something that's been so shameful and hidden, and the presence of a supportive, non-judgemental, and caring therapist can be a very healing experience and can, by itself, correct years of internalised hatred.

Overall, I keep in mind that while the event is in the past, the impacts are right here, right now — and the bulk of the work is in exploring and changing the latter.

When there *are* a range of difficult memories to process, I always recommend that people do so in the presence of another person, ideally a qualified trauma-trained mental health practitioner. Trauma memories can be distressing, and it can be hard to manage the feelings that come up with them; people often need co-regulation to help. Psychologists are trained to support someone in processing these memories, and are attuned and aware of helpful things to say, whereas a lay person might feel overwhelmed or desperately *want* to make things better but inadvertently say something dismissive — 'But it's all okay now!' Psychologists are also trained in helping people manage distress — they won't let someone get flooded with it, and can help a client ground themselves. I especially recommend that people process memories with a psychologist if the abuse involved detachment or dissociation or if it involved significant physical harm, such as sexual or physical abuse.

Some people find solace in journaling or writing. Others may choose to talk to supportive and safe people as a means of seeking care and validation. There's no timeline on processing trauma memories, and experiences may need to be revisited repeatedly, until the meaning has been understood and poison has been leached from the wound.

People often find that once they have adequately discussed and processed some memories, they no longer experience distress when remembering traumatic events. This doesn't mean that the impact on them can be ignored, just that they have reached a certain resolution with it.

Managing trauma impacts

As we explored in chapters 2 and 3, interpersonal trauma can exert huge effects on how we see the world and ourselves, and on our sense of trust, control, and safety.

Understanding characteristic patterns of cognition and emotional responding and learning to amend these is critical work for survivors. Emotions are one of the key psychological senses we use to understand and navigate the world, and without good emotional processing we struggle to respond to the world and to adequately identify and process triggers that indicate danger. Without good emotional processing, we struggle to balance work and other parts of life, to form and make relationships, and to tolerate discomfort in the pursuit of our goals.

Another core part of recovery involves building good relationships and developing the capacity to distinguish between helpful and harmful relationships. Relational traumas, by their very nature, involve wounds that were perpetrated within relationships. As we explored in earlier chapters, this is likely to lead to survivors forming distorted views of relationships.

To start to work on building a good radar, we need to first recognise the ways in which our radar has been impaired, and when we first learnt to excuse or explain harmful behaviours. We can then identify higher-risk situations (e.g., maybe we have no radar with intimate partners, but can pick good friends) and start to actively assess our choices. This doesn't mean that we have to stop interacting with all unsafe people — sometimes we simply can't — but it is a flag that we should stop and think carefully about future interactions or put some buffers in place. Approaching relationships in this way helps avoid the compounding of traumas and helps us develop a greater sense of empowerment, and a calmer and more relationally healthy life.

Living a life of purpose and meaning

Many survivors have a range of issues rendering their lives fundamentally chaotic: trouble with jobs; unstable housing; a lack of hobbies, rest, and play; substance use; dislike of intimacy; a lack of direction and meaning; difficulties making choices or committing to a course of action; difficulties with managing health; severe problems with body image and acceptance; lack of self-compassion; turbulent friendships — these are all common when a survivor begins treatment. They often find that they have not received the scaffolding (i.e., support) that they need around making good lifestyle choices in their early years, and struggle to find any good routine or meaning in life. They may have grown up within families that were abusive or chaotic and neglectful, without any role models who provided consistency, security, and care. Children learn through modelling; if there were no models available to demonstrate things like financial literacy or delayed gratification (i.e., putting off something pleasurable for later gain), they will have grown up without the chance to develop them.

Relational trauma often occurs within systems and contexts that bring chaos. Children who grow up in troubled environments can go on make choices that recreate these environments, either through lack of knowledge, support, and skills or through unconsciously seeking environments that feel familiar. Professionals who work in child protection and justice settings are intimately familiar with this, as they often see case files with patterns replicated across generations. Managing these clients involves supporting them to recognise and understand the difficulties they have, and the psychological patterns and deficits that may underpin them. Sometimes, this work will involve specific future-focused and meaningful goals — such as managing a harmful relationship or finding secure employment — at other times, it will focus on awareness-raising, and slow encouragement to start exploring better structure and limit-setting. This is a difficult pattern as lifestyle chaos often stops someone from accessing supports which can help, such as therapy. Therapists can't work with clients who don't attend treatment, and issues like non-attendance are common with some complex trauma survivors.

Looking beyond the trauma

Many survivors find that the trauma becomes all-consuming and can take over their lives. This is understandable; we'd expect no less when something indescribably difficult, which colours many or all aspects of their life, happens. However, developing an identity that is based purely around being a victim or survivor can inhibit their capacity to do things that are meaningful and to explore joy, freedom, and other parts of their identity (e.g., choir singer, painter, friend). When I work with survivors, I encourage them to remember that they encompass many identities and are capable of amazing and beautiful things. I work with them to create structure, to compartmentalise the trauma-processing, and to actively build identities outside their past experiences, even as we work at chipping away the traumas they carry.

It is necessary to dig down, but it is just as necessary to build up. Most trauma therapies are based on this premise — processing is necessary but is not *sufficient* for a good life. Equally, survivors need to consider how they might find meaning, vocation, play, engagement, and flow in their lives now. None of these things will take away the traumatic events, but they *will* mitigate their impacts and help survivors find more peace and connection in their lives.

Navigating trauma treatment: common mental health difficulties

It's important to have a clear understanding of post-traumatic mental health difficulties so that appropriate treatment can be sought. Myths abound in this space, which leaves survivors vulnerable to unsavoury practitioners looking to capitalise on need. There are a range of therapies, and it is important to match therapy to the difficulty and/ or diagnosis.

By the time Suzie (Chapter 1) came to see me at age 42, she had been diagnosed with borderline personality disorder (BPD), PTSD, generalised anxiety disorder, complex post-traumatic stress disorder (C-PTSD), major depressive disorder, bulimia, and eating disorder not otherwise specified. This is not uncommon. I call this the 'chuck the whole DSM-V' school of diagnosis and it is a signal, for most mental health professionals, of a complex trauma history.

When I'm assessing people, I tend to focus on assessing and understanding *difficulties* — not on finding diagnostic labels that fit. Diagnoses can be helpful as a framework to support understanding and treatment choice, but are essentially artificial, human-made constructs designed to help us impose order. They are not real things, and if they're used without care and consideration, can be unhelpful.

Most survivors have a raft of problems across a few common

domains, including trouble with emotional regulation and management, mood difficulties, hopelessness, anxiety, perfectionism, intrusive thoughts or memories of the trauma, and issues with sleep.

There is a common misconception that the only disorder people are diagnosed with after trauma is PTSD and that any mood difficulties are due to it. But PTSD is a highly specific diagnosis, with specific symptoms, and involves a life-threatening event, either experienced or witnessed (as per the DSM-V diagnostic criteria). The main symptom clusters of PTSD according to the DSM-V include intrusive memories, avoidance of things that remind one of the trauma, negative changes in thinking and mood (e.g., low mood, poor concentration) and changes in physical and emotional reactions (such as hypervigilance). Many people will have subclinical difficulties that do not meet the threshold for this diagnosis. Many complex trauma survivors are also excluded from this diagnosis — as the abuse they faced may not reach the threshold of life-threatening — and are instead likely to have difficulties that align with the diagnoses of BPD, C-PTSD, various mood and anxiety disorders, and impulse control and eating disorders.

C-PTSD is an important diagnosis to discuss. It's not part of the DSM-V, for various complicated reasons, but *is* in the ICD-11 (another diagnostic system) and is becoming increasingly well-recognised as a useful and relevant diagnosis when someone has a relational trauma history. The symptoms involve the classic symptoms of PTSD (i.e., intrusions, avoidance of trauma-related stimuli, and cognitive and affective changes), but also capture many of the other relational and emotional difficulties experienced by complex trauma sufferers, including issues with self-regard (e.g., feeling damaged or worthless), issues with identity, trouble with relationships, physical symptoms (e.g., pain), dissociation, and suicidality. I often find C-PTSD a more comprehensive frame to explain the plethora of difficulties survivors experience, than a list of other diagnoses.

BPD is similar in nature to C-PTSD, but it can occur without trauma (i.e., strong biological and genetic links have been found). Many people with BPD do have a history of trauma underpinning their difficulties, though. The main clinical differences concern the way in which people experience relationships (C-PTSD involves avoidance out of fear, whereas BPD more often involves intense grasping at relationships and strong emotion such as anger when rejection is perceived) and differences in self-regard (C-PTSD involves strong negative views about oneself, while with BPD there is a lack of strong identity). Both BPD and C-PTSD can include difficulties with experiencing intense feelings, relationships that feature deep closeness and rejection, negative appraisals of the world and oneself, impulsivity, difficulties forming an identity, and thoughts of self-harm or suicide. People can have both diagnoses. Survivors may also develop other difficulties, such as: narcissistic personality disorders (often formed as a compensation for the degradation of traumas) and avoidant and dependent personality structures.

Of course, diagnosis is complex, and I have only provided a broad explanation here. But overall, therapy may involve a range of treatments for a multitude of clinical symptoms, based on the unique experiences of the survivor. The emphasis remains on first understanding the nature of the traumatic events and the ensuing problems, and then making sure there are appropriately targeted and multi-systemic supports. This requires a nuanced and careful understanding of a survivor's difficulties, a thorough assessment and diagnostic formulation, and a clear treatment plan. Diagnosis is important insofar as it supports access to treatment, and treatment planning.

Where to find mental health help for trauma?

Navigating the treatment landscape can be tricky. Practitioners and clients alike can miss the trauma underpinning disparate symptoms, and a multitude of unlicensed and unqualified practitioners offer therapies that are, at best, harmless, and at worst, inflict catastrophic damage on an already unsettled psyche.

The explosion in people and professions of all stripes claiming to be able to quickly heal trauma greatly alarms me, especially when I consider the multiple and complex needs of vulnerable survivors and the nature of some of the 'healing' unqualified people offer. Unregulated professionals call themselves counsellors, holistic counsellors, psychotherapists, life coaches, energy healers, shamans, reiki practitioners, soul-healers, Christian therapists — all of which are unregulated professions in Australia, leaving their clients unprotected. Anyone can give themselves one of these titles and start a business, with zero qualifications, experience, training, or oversight. Many of these professions require no formal mental health training or qualifications. While there are some doing excellent work (notably, well-trained and experienced counsellors and psychotherapists), it is near impossible to know how to find appropriately trained professionals.

I have worked with many survivors who are confused about where to find help or who struggle to know what types of help are available or suitable. By the time most of them enter the offices of a trauma-trained clinician, they've often been taking mood medication for years, have attracted a few diagnoses, and will usually have seen several therapists, with varying degrees of success. Each unsuccessful episode of treatment can lead to a deeper sense of failure.

'I feel like I even failed at therapy,' a client once said to me. She had spent several years seeing a counsellor who engaged in energy healing work and past-life regression, but felt somewhat reassured when I explained that she'd not even *begun* proper trauma therapy.

There are many excellent practitioners and therapies available, but it's crucial to first recognise your difficulties as trauma-related, and then seek appropriate help.

Broadly speaking, psychiatrists, psychologists, and mental health/clinical social workers are the most common mental health professionals in Australia, the United States, and the United Kingdom. These professions are overseen by regulatory bodies — such as the Australian Health Practitioners Regulation Agency (AHPRA) — and require registration with national agencies. This ensures consistency of care, basic standards of training and professional practice, and a code of ethics that practitioners must adhere to. Practitioners operate in public mental health services, and privately; the former largely being reserved for clients with severe mental health disorders.

At present, in Australia, Medicare provides individuals with up to 20 sessions of subsidised psychological therapy, if they have a referral from a GP. This used to be ten sessions, which is manifestly inadequate for treating most serious mental health conditions (especially trauma) but was increased to 20 in the wake of COVID-19 — it remains to be seen how long this will last. In the United Kingdom, psychiatrists and licensed clinical psychologists dominate, and access to therapy is often via the National Health Service (NHS). In the United States, treatment is offered privately and via networks of providers who contract with managed-care organisations, by state-licensed professionals, including psychiatrists, psychologists, clinical social workers, and professional counsellors.

Psychiatrists are highly trained medical professionals who can also prescribe medication. While there is no medication for trauma per se (i.e., nothing that will remove all the difficulties with feelings, thinking, and behavioural patterns), medication can be helpful in managing emotionality, low mood, anxiety, nightmares, or insomnia. I often work in tandem with psychiatric colleagues and GPs to provide a wraparound service to clients with complex needs. GPs are the linchpin of health services in Australia, and I thank my lucky stars — and cling on for dear life — when I find one with an interest in mental health and a compassionate approach.

Psychologists and clinical social workers are trained in talking therapies, i.e., therapies that will involve talking and collaboratively understanding the trauma and its effects. The most tested and validated treatments for PTSD are prolonged exposure (PE), cognitive processing therapy (CPT) for PTSD, and eye movement desensitisation and reprocessing (EMDR). Imagery-rescripting for PTSD is another promising treatment, but it is still being tested. CPT involves reworking beliefs that keep people stuck in trauma recovery (e.g., 'he raped me because I was wearing a short skirt', or 'I can't trust any men now') and with building good emotional expression and management. EMDR and PE both involve discussing the trauma with the therapist following a specific protocol, which allows the brain to rewire how it processes and holds these memories and trauma-related cognitions. PE involves long periods of exposure to trauma memories from different angles, while EMDR involves short bursts of exposure as someone also focuses on bilateral stimulation (e.g., a therapist moving their fingers in front of someone's eyes). The theory is that taxing someone's working memory in this manner with split focus allows the brain to process and integrate trauma memories.

For interpersonal and complex trauma presentations, schema therapy and dialectical behaviour therapy (DBT) can also be very useful. I have discussed schema therapy previously and use it a lot in my own practice, though it is not a trauma-specific therapy and those with specific PTSD diagnoses need other treatment. DBT works well for those with severe emotional regulation or interpersonal problems (such as with BPD diagnoses) and involves skills-building work, and training in mindfulness and interpersonal competencies. Most therapists use a mixture of these therapies, though certain therapies like CPT and PE must be used in line with a specific protocol. Some people will also gain benefit from trauma-focused cognitive behavioural therapy (TF-CBT), attachment-based therapies, or acceptance and commitment therapy (ACT). Overall, treating complex trauma requires relatively intense and longer-term work, and necessitates the use of a range of interventions tailored to address each client's unique needs.

There is no better or worse therapy (within reason), and the choice should be made collaboratively, with a solid understanding of a client's issues, preferences, and relational style. For instance, I would be more likely to use a CBT-based approach for clients who are driven by logic, with presenting issues such as identifiable anxiety with certain triggers, while clients with deep early wounding and relational issues might be better suited to schema therapy. With other clients who have PTSD co-morbid with other diagnoses, I start with a PTSD-specific treatment like CPT and then move into another type of therapy after the protocol to 'mop up' the remaining symptoms.

The crux is that trauma requires targeted therapy, not non-directive general counselling. Most skilled practitioners will be able to merge elements of certain therapies (though there are some who choose to work exclusively with a certain modality).

Sensorimotor therapies focusing on using the body and movement to heal are becoming increasingly popular, from the well-studied and researched (yoga) to the somewhat more esoteric and poorly established (such as rebirthing). Well-established approaches can be excellent for some clients, and can be a great support for healing. However, as trauma creates fractures in the ways people think, understand, and process, language-based strategies to aid insight and change remain my primary therapeutic choices. I do use sensorimotor approaches within this framework — such as polyvagal activation to help people soothe themselves when distressed (the polyvagal system is the body's natural regulatory system and activates and calms — modulating this system has become a well-recognised part of trauma therapy) — but rely in the main on well-researched psychological talking approaches. I encourage people to engage in body work as well, if they express an interest in this, but steer them towards established and safe modalities, and away from the wilder and whackier fringes of the 'healing' landscape. Some of my clients engage in other forms of therapy —gardening therapy, music and art therapies, equine therapy, and yoga — which can all be excellent aids.

Trauma therapy is usually best engaged in consistently, with regular, frequent appointments. I prefer to see most of my relational trauma clients on a weekly or fortnightly basis, at the same time each week where possible. Life has often been chaotic for them and providing consistency can be helpful. I'm flexible with clients as needed — not everyone has lots of spare time, and money to spend — but also encourage them to give themselves the best chance at healing by committing to regular therapy.

Finding safety in a therapist

Relational traumas involve boundary crossing, and some survivors will have difficulty with differentiating between safe and unsafe practitioners, and end up seeing therapists who cross boundaries and compound the initial trauma. I have known survivors who have been sexually victimised by therapists, who have seen therapists practising a range of therapies that have never been tested (e.g., past life regression, reiki), and who have accidentally joined cults in the pursuit of healing. Likewise, I've seen practitioners who offer too much out of a desire to rescue and then quickly become overwhelmed and withdraw, and practitioners who behave like perpetrators (e.g., becoming angry and blaming).

I offer below a set of guidelines for identifying a safe therapist. This list is (perhaps understandably) biased towards the ethics that psychologists usually adhere to, but it can also be applied to other types of therapy with some tweaks. I provide these guidelines as a framework of things to consider, not as an exhaustive list.

A good therapist will be able to tell you about their qualifications, experience, and the types of therapy they practise. Ideally, they would be registered health practitioners and governed by a professional body. They will be collaborative and take your wishes into account. They will seek informed consent for anything they suggest, with a very small handful of exceptions, such as if you are actively suicidal or psychotic and they need to ensure you are protected. I have this discussion clearly with my clients at the outset — I can't do therapy with a dead client and the agreement my clients must accept is that I will do my best to keep them safe and alive.

A good practitioner will refer you on to someone else if they feel they can't meet your needs. They will be able to provide feedback about the nature of your difficulties and where these difficulties have come from. They will be able to explain which therapeutic modalities they recommend, and why. There should be a good research evidence base for the therapy they suggest, and they should know this evidence and be willing to talk you through it if asked. A good practitioner will be honest — even if this is challenging sometimes.

A good practitioner will never touch you without your consent (most psychiatrists, psychologists, and social workers should never touch you). Having said this, I have younger clients who like doing fist bumps or similar on the way in and out of a session, and I allow this — it feels like a safe form of touch, and to deny it could seem like a rejection and cause more harm than it's worth. Other practitioners will touch clients to provide bilateral stimulation for EMDR (e.g., tapping on knees), to provide soothing (e.g., a hand on shoulder), or for health checks (such as a psychiatrist might conduct). Touch should always occur only if clinically indicated, and with full consent.

A good therapist will only practise within the scope of their knowledge and training. A psychologist should not offer dietary advice (beyond the basics), unless they also have qualifications as a dietitian.

A good practitioner will have clearly defined boundaries: they will be able to tell you their expectations of you (e.g., regular attendance as agreed), their availability, their capacity to respond to crises, and whether/how to make contact between sessions. Trauma survivors need practitioners with well-articulated and reasonable boundaries — it's hard work for both parties, and it's essential that therapists take care of themselves outside of work to be fully available in session. It's unfortunately common for practitioners to extend themselves too much, and then burn out and reject clients. While boundaries can sometimes feel like they are there to keep a client out, they are really in place to keep a therapist's energy in, so that they can be fully present over a long period of time. Good boundaries also help ensure that a therapist is objective, and that they maintain a separation between their personal life and work. A client must never be used to meet a therapist's psychological or physical needs (beyond the exchange of a fee for time) — which means that therapists need enough time and energy outside work to get all their needs met elsewhere. As someone who often collapses spent on the couch after a day of therapy work, I can profess that this is a hard ask. Good boundaries should be flexible as far as possible at times of increased distress or need. However, trauma survivors can often have very chaotic lives and it is important for therapists not to get caught up in the chaos but to gently and firmly hold their own limits. This can mean simple things such as sticking to appointment times if someone runs late or putting boundaries around phone calls or behaviour in session (e.g., no substance use before or during session).

A good therapist will be able to take responsibility for difficulties that arise in the room and will apologise when necessary. I remember well the first (and only) time I became truly angry with my therapist. It was shortly before Christmas, and she had just told me that she was going away on a three-week break. This doesn't seem like a lot anymore, but it felt interminable at the time, given the intensity of the work we were doing, and I became quite upset at the lack of notice, but also the abandonment I felt. She was able to own her role in it (i.e., she did not apologise for going away on leave, as that was very much her right, but did apologise for not giving me enough notice). This was a powerful moment for me, as my experiences in other relationships had hitherto largely involved emotional invalidation (i.e., being told that my feelings were wrong). Being able to express my anger and have it acknowledged felt like a turning point. I try to give my clients the same gift of an acknowledgement and apology when I stuff up.

Finally, a good therapist will be imperfect (i.e., they will likely make mistakes at some stage), but overall will be sensitive, authentic, and usually leave a client feeling heard and validated. I say usually, because therapy may involve tricky moments and times of invalidation. These sometimes occur because of misunderstandings or mistakes in session, but can also occur because a client has particular patterns of relating and interpreting, which they bring into the therapy room. It is almost always helpful and powerful to let a therapist know when we experience difficult feelings about something they've said. A good therapist will work with us to help us understand the patterns. A good therapist will also challenge someone when appropriate, though this should never involve shame or aggression.

The clinical tasks for a therapist are manifold: to undertake appropriate training across a range of trauma-treatment modalities; to learn to accurately assess trauma and to build a map of impacts; to determine the most relevant treatment targets; to learn to share complex clinical information in an accessible manner; to give clients a choice of treatments and some agency with the pacing of treatment; to learn to advocate for clients in an oft-uncaring system; and to build competencies in skilful and sensitive interpersonal communication, especially when working with clients who might be quick to perceive rejection or insult.

The personal tasks for a therapist are likewise varied: to take responsibility, but not all of it; to steer a client without directing them; to hold boundaries but to be able to be flexible with those boundaries when truly warranted; to own one's own reactions and responses in an honest, authentic, and forthright manner; to be exquisitely attuned to in-the-room processes and manage difficult conversations with grace; to accept and to challenge; to understand one's own responses to different clients; to ensure that one has adequate personal supports, including personal therapy, to manage the weight of the work being done; to carefully balance a caseload of clients to avoid overwhelming oneself; to learn to be authentic; and, most importantly, to be okay with failing, and model the inevitability and acceptability of being imperfect to one's clients — including at all the tasks listed above.

Managing and treating trauma is truly a paradox — a move between the past and the present, between unconditional acceptance and the need for change, between support and a gentle nudge out of the nest, between kindness and honesty. I hope that treating clinicians and clients alike can hold in mind the life-changing value of the task being undertaken, and can go gently, with hope, resilience, and care.

5

The Difficult
Trauma Victim

Not all trauma victims are likeable, and it is easy for us to forget — or ignore — that some difficult people are very hurt people. As I said at the outset of this book, my work has led me to the darker corners of the treatment landscape, and I consider it essential to include discussion of the more harmful behaviours that can signal a history of trauma. Many people with severe trauma histories find themselves embroiled in difficult behaviours that can lead to consequences such as incarceration. The clients I have worked with in public forensic mental health services and correctional facilities are some of the most damaged individuals I have ever seen, but they remain invisible to most. These individuals are truly hurt but many of them are also *very* difficult for clinicians and systems to treat and manage. When I say 'difficult trauma victim', I don't mean to be pejorative — it is, instead, a frank and honest reflection of how some victims display their pain, how we view them, and the ways in which systems tend to treat them.

When I think of a 'difficult' victim, I most often think of Kate. My therapy with her did not have an auspicious start. Prisons in Victoria took COVID-19 very seriously, and while I was pleased that they made such efforts to protect the vulnerable prison population, it also meant that I wore goggles and an N-95 mask all the time, allowing clients to only see a tiny slice of my face. It also meant waves of repeated lockdowns (where prisoners were locked into their cells for 24 hours a day), exacerbating mental health issues and distress for most people.

Interestingly, most of my clients adapted to not being able to see my face, and didn't seem to miss many of the bodily and facial cues I use to communicate empathy in sessions — while I became an expert at using exaggerated eyebrow swoops and thespian smiles to communicate, as well as modulating my voice to signal certain emotions.

The goggles and mask were not the only barrier between my clients and me. During our first session, one client — Kate — sat handcuffed inside a floor-to-ceiling wire enclosure in the outdoor yard of her management unit, while I sat outside the enclosure, perched on a plastic chair the prison officers had placed there for me. The sun was shining, but Kate was in the shadow of the ten-foot walls surrounding her. I realised that I was effectively doing therapy with someone inside a cage. There are certain moments in my career when I wonder about the career choices I have made, the choices we have all collectively made, and about the tortured psyches our civilisation has given birth to, which we must now manage the best we can — this was one of those moments.

Nevertheless, forensic psychologists are an adaptable bunch, so I soldiered on. The rest of the session was unremarkable, perhaps notable only for how tangential Kate was; her mind free-ranged from one topic to the next, and she asked me several probing and inappropriate questions, blithely disregarding normal professional boundaries. I was aware of how tense I was, and how carefully I had to think through my answers, allowing her some knowledge of me, but carefully establishing boundaries while also watching to see if these boundaries were perceived by her as rejection. When Kate felt rejected or provoked, she assaulted people.

Kate had spent much of her life bouncing in and out of prison and between various services. She had a range of serious mental health difficulties and a very severe abuse history commencing at birth. There were few types of abuse that had not been perpetrated against her, and all her caregivers had severely hurt her. She was an inferno of rage. She was childlike in her presentation, with the same propensity to quick anger that a two-year-old might display — but with the dangers of a sharper, street-smart mind, a history of volatility, a predilection for making (and using) weapons, and an adult-sized body.

I was anxious, and for good reason. Kate was placed in a management unit[1] (a unit designed for careful control of prisoners, with strict protocols around access to the broader compound) after severely assaulting a range of people. Everyone was anxious about who she would hurt next. The management unit was old and grim, with entry through a forbidding steel gate locked with a padlock — very different to the biometric swipe entry to the sleek foyer of the newly built mental health unit I spent most of my time in. It was dark inside, and the lino was worn and peeling, with scuff marks on the walls. The foyer held monitors visible to all walking into the unit. These monitors beamed CCTV from the observation cells, where women placed on 'obs' regimes (most often for suicide and mental health reasons) ate, slept, showered, toileted, and attended to their menstrual needs in clear view of everyone — staff, visitors to the unit, and tradespeople alike — dressed in sleeveless canvas smocks. The lack of carpet and acoustic proofing meant that the shouts of the women echoed back and forth down the hallway, folding into a cacophony. The hallway was winged with steel doors with ventilation grills on the bottom — allowing staff to talk to prisoners without opening the door. Each door had a piece of cloth tacked over the observation window, perhaps to provide some privacy, as well as an A4 sheet of paper with each prisoner's name. Sometimes the women shouted to each other and sometimes they just shouted. I often thought that I would go quite mad if I worked there. In these grim environs lived some of the most disturbed women I had ever met.

Kate was escorted in and out of her cell in the presence of specially trained staff. This didn't allow us much privacy, as we were always observed through a glass door, but when I sat across from Kate in a tiny interview room a few weeks later as her face darkened with rage, I was grateful for the watchful eye of these correctional officers. She had a history of assaulting people both in the community and in prison, and she had limited capacity to manage her impulses. She was quick to perceive hostility and so attuned to any sign of rejection or anger that she responded with aggression and violence to any limit-setting. She was a long-term management patient, and the correctional system was worried about her ability to reintegrate into the community, as well as how to manage her risk in prison.

Kate divided people. Some people struggled to see her as dangerous and focused on her extensive and terrible trauma history. 'Victim, not perpetrator', is a common narrative, and in this case is no doubt influenced by our instinctive aversion to believing that women can harm. Paradoxically, while this is helpful to some women — who can retain their victim identity despite the harms they inflict — for others it means that they are hated far more violently than any man who commits similar offences. Some of my female clients who had hurt or killed their children experienced this, as they were called 'monsters', 'crazed killers', and similar epithets, even though most often these offences occurred when they were struggling with serious mental illnesses, which caused (or contributed to) what they did. 'Look me up online and see what they said about me,' one client said. I did — but wished I hadn't.

Management or solitary confinement regimes are used to contain those who are at risk of harming themselves or other people, and these behaviours are most often underpinned by severe personality dysfunction, psychiatric illnesses, acquired brain injuries/intellectual disabilities, polysubstance use, and extensive histories of serious trauma, which have often warped beyond recognition the way a person perceives and responds to the world. In some instances, these regimes are the only ways in which people can be managed safely in existing environments without staff being assaulted. There are a number of people like Kate in the correctional and forensic mental health system, people who have intense abuse histories that would be unfathomable to most of us and have developed a range of methods of coping with the associated distress — often by harming themselves or harming other people.

Kate turned to self-harm as a way of managing and expressing difficult feelings and had spent significant time on suicide watch. Her trauma history was one of the most severe I had heard, and began when she was just a baby. Most of us cannot begin to imagine the depths of terror and betrayal she likely experienced, and how this shaped her personality and psychological defences into a finely honed attack missile — sensing danger and attacking before she was attacked. The binary in her mind was neat — prey or be preyed upon — though she didn't have the capacity or vocabulary to articulate this.

People can be both victims and perpetrators, and while Kate was a victim of some truly horrific abuses first, the abuses she suffered had distorted her personality structure. All the normal human mechanisms of being had warped in her, such that she had built a towering rage and hatred of all that was human. The tiny percentage of vulnerability she maintained was hidden behind a defence of believing that she was entitled to do as she wished to other people. Weakness was anathema to her — she hated it in other people, and she likely hated most the young Kate who was once so vulnerable. Trauma-informed work was important, but it would not fundamentally change the predator she had now become. It was unlikely that treatment would succeed in altering her personality structure, and at best we hoped for a change in how she expressed her anger, while focusing on environmental containment and management strategies (e.g., supported accommodation upon release).

It's important to talk about the fact that women can be perpetrators of harm too, whether psychological or physical. I have worked with women who have engaged in all forms of interpersonal harm — bullying, emotional abuse, intimate partner violence, child neglect, physical and child sex abuse (though it *is* quite rare for women to perpetrate sexual abuse), physical violence, and murder. Women more commonly engage in practices that are psychologically harmful, such as bullying and emotional abuse. Women offend less frequently than men, and often for slightly different reasons, with mental health difficulties and social factors including trauma histories, family, and intimate relationships taking on greater significance,[2] though there are also many similarities to the beliefs, personalities, and psychological factors that underlie male-perpetrated harm.

Most of the violent female offenders I have worked with have truly horrific trauma histories that have fundamentally altered their identity structures by the time they start offending. What's clear to me after encountering them is that we cannot discount women as possible sources of harm. We must pay attention to the unique factors underlying their circumstances, we must consider trauma-informed and perpetrator-informed interventions and systems — but we also need to understand the attitudes, beliefs, and character traits held by most people who harm. Our efforts must be aimed at both understanding and preventing abuse, regardless of who perpetrates it.

Many women in the forensic system were victims first, and then became perpetrators. It is essential, but difficult, to see both. Some people are biased towards seeing women only as victims, and believe that women only hurt others if they are traumatised. Some firmly believe that once a person hurts someone, they become a perpetrator only. Both these dichotomies are false; in clinical work, one must straddle these two poles and provide victim-specific and trauma-informed care, while keeping sight of the importance of stopping harmful behaviour and protecting other people.

Stepping down from management regimes usually requires some measure of behaviour change as well as tolerance of the risk a client poses — and correctional environments are notoriously risk-averse. I understood this — if Kate harmed another prisoner or a staff member as she was tested out of management, the prison would be liable. Staff members must be safe where they work and occupational violence *must* be minimised, even in a setting such as a prison or a forensic hospital. I have worked with peers who have been assaulted by clients, and the toll it takes on the professional can be massive, sometimes causing PTSD in the professionals themselves. Even where a physical assault doesn't happen, behaviours such as threats or verbal aggression are common, and can cause great stress. Balancing Kate's needs with those of all the staff working with her, and those of her co-prisoners, was difficult. However, people who go straight from long-term management regimes into the community often struggle to adjust and tend to quickly reoffend, returning to prison and lurching into the same cycle.

The systems around a person as complex as Kate usually start to mirror the internal chaos of the person. We had multiple meetings and conferences about her, trying various treatments and failing, circling back and through various intervention and management ideas, with little progress. She was stuck, and we were stuck. This was not her fault, and it certainly didn't mean we didn't *want* to help her, but rather that the complexities of her needs and the intractability of some of her behaviours made resolution difficult. It also highlighted how difficult and frustrating it can feel to try to help someone, when their idea of what help is diverges from other people's views, and they have seemingly little interest in the painstaking plans laid out by the services working with them. There was an inherent opposition between Kate's desire for more freedom, her behaviours, and the system's need to keep other people safe; and this was hard to navigate.

Kate was ambivalent about her time in prison. She often declared that she wanted to be back in the outside world, but a part of her liked the containment of her unit. She had settled well into life there — with her art, some study, and a regular routine — and often refused to engage in the steps she needed to transition out of the unit. This was perhaps the most stable her life had been, and the doors that locked her in also locked harmful people out. The world had not been kind to her, and it was sad to see how much more contained and settled she was in prison. There are a handful of Kates in the world I inhabit, and it wouldn't be inaccurate to say that experiences of trauma sit at the foundation of their difficulties.

I am not suggesting that prison is positive, either — incarceration has significant negative effects for many people, and behaviours can often be far better changed through a judicious mix of treatment, wraparound supports, a focus on basics such as housing and health, and supervision in the community. Incarceration is used as a blunt weapon, and certain communities — such as the Aboriginal community in Australia — have disproportionate rates of incarceration, pointing to social problems that should be addressed through other means. It would not be remiss to note that Australia is a carceral nation and that people easily bay for blood and scream 'just lock them up', without consideration or care about the harms that incarceration can cause, sometimes for generations. While Kate had found a measure of containment in prison, many prisoners find that they are accidentally retraumatised or worse, are outright abused in a state-sanctioned manner in prisons and other detention facilities.

Nevertheless, there *are* some people who are unable to arrest the circuits of difficulty their lives inhabit, and prison (in the absence of other supportive-but-contained environments) can sometimes act as a circuit breaker for harmful behaviours, or as a safety blanket for those who are truly violent and psychopathic — protecting other people and themselves from these dark impulses. There are others who need the firm limits certain environments provide, and cannot find similar services in the community in our current era of defunding.

My assessment of Kate was that she was severely traumatised, with difficulties spanning generations. Her troubles started a long time before her birth, and it is likely that her course was somewhat inevitable. It is common for complex relational traumas to occur intergenerationally — to put it very simply, hurt people hurt people. It's unlikely that a mother who beats and tries to kill her child has had a safe and happy upbringing. Similarly, it is unlikely that that mother's parents, in turn, were loved and secure. Thus, we can trace trauma back through generations, sometimes reducing in intensity over time — usually only once it is recognised, named, and treated — but more often compounding.

Fractured attachments and abuse at the earliest stages of life completely change the way a person perceives and understands the world. A baby's brain is a sponge, a blob of amorphous grey matter, and they learn furiously in the first few years of their lives through observing other people. They learn language, the shapes and sounds of the world, attachment, attention, self-soothing, empathy, and how to be human. When parents have severe trauma histories themselves, they are often unable to provide anything a baby needs to learn about the world. They were never parented themselves and are swept up in the distress and chaos of their own lives — at best, ignoring their children; at worst, actively abusing them.

I have worked with people who were left lying in cots alone for days on end, developing none of the motor, relational, or cognitive skills that babies usually would. They emerged from key developmental periods with none of this essential learning, and with a pre-verbal terror at having been left alone and the primal recognition that it could have resulted in their death. Even a benign neglect — because parents are preoccupied with mental illness, substance use, or fulfilling the basic needs of life — can have malignant effects on a child's idea of themselves and the world, as well as on their regulatory capacities. 'People are bad, I am bad, I will always be hurt, no one will be there for me, attack first, take what you need, never trust' — these are some of the beliefs that people such as Kate and Madison formed, and they're encoded at deep, non-verbal levels. These same people lack the ability to self-soothe and regulate their impulses and feelings, and these internal templates set the scene for how they behave.

Some very traumatised people even turn their intense anger and anguish onto their own bodies, gouging and burning themselves, disembowelling themselves, inserting objects into various bodily orifices, and swallowing foreign objects. Self-harm can serve a regulatory function for some trauma victims, as the endorphins released through pain can calm people; it can also be used as a way of telegraphing distress, of seeking care, and of punishing oneself. Over time, these self-harm behaviours become a person's primary means of expression and coping, and can eventually result in fatalities. Managing and reducing this behaviour is an essential part of work with some victims, and it can be difficult to get people to relinquish a well-formed coping mechanism and replace it with more adaptive expressions of distress. These behaviours can be stigmatised and are sometimes mistakenly brushed away as 'attention-seeking' by health services involved in the care of these individuals.

I empathise with the health services; it is challenging to try to heal someone only for them to immediately engage in acts that run counter to your attempts — especially if you're not given support to understand their underlying anguish. The ways in which some professionals deal with this, though — sewing up self-harm wounds without anaesthesia, or placing suicidal people alone in isolation cells with no stimulation, both of which commonly occur — inflicts unnecessary psychological pain, dehumanises individuals, and often mirrors the initial traumas.

When I worked with adolescents under child protection care in my pre-psychologist days, we had a very troubled young woman placed with us. She engaged in very serious forms of self-harm, including placing large metal objects inside her arm, spraying blood everywhere in the process. She did this all in a dispassionate, somewhat detached manner, with no obvious signs of emotion, apart from mild amusement at the horrified responses of her carers. The ambulance services often attended the house multiple times a day, becoming ever more fatigued and annoyed as they bandaged up her wounds, only for her to rip the bandages and stitches off as soon as they left. This young girl was (*was*, because she died by suicide a few years later) severely disturbed — on reflection, I believe she would have benefited from assertive mental health interventions to assess, understand, contain, and manage her behaviours.

Unfortunately, child and adolescent mental health services are woefully underfunded in most states in Australia with many cracks in the system, and this girl fell through all of them. She refused care, and would not even talk to a psychologist on an outpatient basis. Her behaviours were left to be managed (with heroic, but untrained efforts by agencies involved in her care) in the community. I am not suggesting that earlier and more comprehensive mental health intervention would have saved her life — sometimes people are so distressed that they choose to die despite all attempts to intervene — but it would have at least given her a chance, and a more informed choice.

Some of the adults I have worked with in the correctional system were once babies who were methamphetamine-affected in the womb; others have foetal alcohol spectrum disorders (FASD), damaging their neurological development before birth, with resultant difficulties with impulsivity, anger, or self-regulation. The biological, social, and psychological cohere in a dangerous mix. Some babies were abused by their parents or those close to their parents; were raped and prostituted by their own families; flung against walls; hit, stripped, thrashed, cut, and burnt. Some of my clients had stakes and nails hammered into them by their caregivers for punishment. Others were made sexually available to a revolving door of their mother's partners or were forced to engage in sexual acts with their own siblings, or the family pet. Yet others were shaken in fits of rage, bruising their tender brains. Some were introduced to drugs by their parents at the age of four — an age when we are just beginning to lose our milk teeth. Some of them had parents who were part of the Stolen Generations, who continued to reel from the impacts of being ripped away from all they knew, and the devastation of being removed from their kin and their lands.

Against this canvas, already battered beyond recognition, we can add on layers of troubling experiences — emotional abuse, difficulties at school (many children with significant trauma histories have trouble focusing and managing the behavioural expectations of normal schools), bullying, rejection by peers, early substance use, school disengagement, intense anger and difficulties managing this explosive rage, few occupational choices, very poor physical health by mid-adulthood, poor emotional management, difficult relationships characterised by abuse and violence, incarceration — and a repeat of this cycle when these hurt children become adults and partner up with people who are similarly hurt, and have their own babies.

We know this story well in the forensic world, and it is a devastatingly sad one.

Kate *was* a victim — but one of the more difficult ones. When we think of trauma, we often focus our attention on those whose symptoms are socially acceptable — those who might develop anxiety or depression, PTSD, or other internalising behaviours (i.e., directed towards oneself). We prefer to ignore the significant proportion of externalising (i.e., directed outward) or harmful behaviours that are also underpinned by trauma.

I am not suggesting that all harm and violence is caused by trauma. Most victims will never hurt anyone else, but certain types of harms *can* result in a survivor developing a personality structure and psychosocial difficulties that lead to harm being caused to others.

We have neat binaries in our minds: victims and perpetrators. Some people are both, and we struggle to know where to place these people and how to respond to them. Perhaps we want to ignore the types of harms people like Kate have faced because they are so unpalatable; perhaps the task feels too monumental. Perhaps at some stage we have moved into seeing the Kates of this world as perpetrators, forgetting they are also victims. Perhaps we only see them as victims, forgetting the harm they have caused. Essentially, working with trauma victims who are so fundamentally damaged requires the capacity to hold *both* views in mind, while trying to create systems that contain and protect everyone.

6

Why People Harm

My first class in forensic psychology during my doctoral degree transformed my views on offending. While it involved no seminal client work, it slowly rippled through the rest of my training, changing how I thought about the infliction of harm. Our lecturer started class by asking us simply to reflect on the last time we had broken a law — and to consider why.

I smiled to myself; this was easy. I am often lax with following parking restrictions — born of a certain optimism and misplaced faith in my capacity to evade parking inspectors — and a general desire to get on with the excitement of life. I thought about the ways in which I explained this to myself ('It doesn't really matter', 'It doesn't hurt anyone,' 'They are silly revenue-raising laws anyway', 'I can't be bothered moving my car in the rain').

'Think carefully about the ways in which you just justified your actions to yourself,' our lecturer said. 'Those are no different to the rationalisations your clients will make about their actions.'

While the acts I engaged in were far less serious than the acts my clients engage in, at their core were the same thoughts and beliefs: an entitlement to breach limits that I did not consider relevant to my own life; a stimulation-seeking personality; and a higher tolerance for risk than the average person. This is, I must add, the same personality structure that means I thrive in forensic work and can balance a range of competing work priorities. We all have a range of personality traits, and each trait comes with positives and drawbacks. Awareness and insight are key, not attempting to be 'perfect' people with perfect behaviour.

Over time, I have seen repeatedly how similar people who harm are to those who do not harm: there are only slight differences in personal histories, the severity of certain traits (i.e., we can be somewhat self-centred, or very self-centred, with vastly different outcomes), and the presence of various social structures that facilitate or inhibit certain behaviours.

I remain fascinated by our cultural obsession with crime, its antecedents, and our motivations for it. True crime and crime fiction genres have exploded in popularity as we collectively plumb the depths of the human psyche. I love these genres myself, often choosing to curl up with a good crime thriller after a day in prison. I usually laugh to myself as I do — the motives and types of crimes featured in these books are chalk from cheese in comparison to the daily grind of immersion in the forensic world.

The reality for people who offend is not often born of fantastic psychological twists and dark desires, but instead of the mundane: crushing need; anger; secret fears; repressing instead of confronting; trying to control a world that seems dangerous and out of control; avoidance; hostility; difficulties with communicating (and thus showing instead of telling). Harms and abuse are often born of a mixture of these few ingredients.

A quick look at popular psychological websites would instead have me believe that most people who abuse others inhabit a world unknown to the rest of us. The 'us' and 'them' are clearly delineated, with 'them' being labelled psychopaths and narcissists, or monsters of some shape and form. While there *is* some truth in the idea that personality traits influence harmful behaviours and there certainly are some true sadists, psychopaths, and narcissists, the reality is far more prosaic. My view of offending and the perpetration of harm is vastly different to the neat explanations often shared.

Most professionals who operate within the clinical and legal spaces with perpetrators share this view and understand the many and varied reasons that lead people to perpetrate harm; the common trajectories that often underlie perpetration and the ubiquity of harmful behaviours. The reality is that many of us will engage in harmful behaviours at times, and it's important not to set people up as heroes or villains. Our current culture seems built on idealising certain people and placing them on a pedestal, and then just as quickly ripping them down and apart. This is a harmful pattern, as it blinds us to the essential inconsistencies and frailties in human nature.

People harm other people for a whole range of reasons: very few of them have a clinical diagnosis of narcissistic personality disorder. Even fewer are true psychopaths, who are extremely rare, typically under 1 per cent of the general population,[1] and even relatively rare in a prison setting. I have only met a handful of psychopaths in my work, and none in my personal life.

Psychopathy is a construct far broader and more detailed than the casual way we use it ('He is so cold, he must be a psychopath';'If you drink gin, you might be a psychopath') and involves attitudes, behaviours, and affective responses that are geared towards the callous, unemotional, reckless, glib, impulsive, and irresponsible. People may have certain traits of psychopathy, but most people who harm other people will not do so merely out of a fundamental disregard for the needs and feelings of other people — there will be other factors involved. Similarly, narcissistic personality disorder is relatively rare (0.5–5 per cent[2] of the general population, though more common in clinical settings) and interpersonal harm is very rarely underpinned purely by narcissistic traits, though these traits can be a factor.

Why does this seemingly semantic difference matter?

It matters because unless we can understand — carefully, truthfully, and bravely — the reasons someone harms, we cannot treat or manage these behaviours, and they will continue.

In this chapter, I will draw from the forensic psychological and clinical literature, with a specific emphasis on the excellent body of work already done by colleagues at the Problem Behaviour Program, Forensicare,[3] and the Centre for Forensic Behavioural Science, Swinburne, to explore the origin of interpersonal harms and difficult behaviours. This chapter is not geared towards understanding theories of crime, but rather, focused on helping readers understand those who abuse. Criminological and forensic theories are vast and complex, and I have focused on distilling this large and learned body of work into something relatively digestible for all, but which is based on sound knowledge, not on clickbait or entertainment. Any errors or omissions are mine alone.

Some of the harms I discuss are criminal (e.g., sex offending, violence, stalking) while others reside in the grey area between harmful and illegal (e.g., bullying, emotional abuse, intrusive behaviours, online harassment).

Most harmful behaviours occur on a spectrum from less to more severe. This scale refers to *physical* damage only — it's not intended to scale traumas as either more or less psychologically damaging. Rape is at the extreme end of the harm scale: it often involves a strong sense of entitlement, including entitlement to breach another person's bodily integrity. At the less severe end of the scale, we see other behaviours involving violation of bodily integrity, such as insisting that a friend use drugs against their will or trying to talk a partner into having sex though they've said they don't want to. This is very different from discussing sexual needs within a relationship and negotiating this terrain with a partner. The latter is respectful and helpful, and is very different from trying to coerce or guilt a partner into having sex when they have already said no. In the middle of the scale are behaviours such as a parent smacking a child, with severe physical abuse sliding up towards the top of the scale.

There are a range of emotionally harmful behaviours that can similarly be mapped on a scale, such as bullying, emotional abuse, online trolling, and harassment. These behaviours are harmful, too, and can also be understood using the framework I present in this chapter. As we explored in the victimisation chapters, the *meaning* and *frequency* of events are what influences the traumatic response, not the severity of the event alone.

Each of these behaviours involves different levels of physical and psychological harm, but all are fundamentally underpinned by attitudes including:

a. privilege of one's own needs and emotions over those of another, and

b. entitlement to the bodily choices and space of another person.

People do not always move along the spectrum (i.e., it is not a slippery slope). Most of us have a set point in our attitudes — we may consider some of the less harmful behaviours acceptable but are horrified at the thought of raping or assaulting someone. It's useful to notice our attitudes. As an example, do we think it's okay for a parent to hit a child? What makes violence acceptable in this instance, but not in others?

It's important to note this spectrum, so we can become aware of problematic attitudes and break down the myth that there is some magical thinking that sets abusive people apart from the rest of us. We are *all* likely to engage in some of these behaviours at different points in time, and insight (without self-blame) is critical to helping us become more respectful people.

Understanding harmful behaviour

When we consider behaviour, it is helpful to remember a few basic principles. First, few behaviours are truly arbitrary.

Every behaviour is used as a means of communication, and as a way of either gaining a desired outcome or avoiding an unwanted one. If we can keep this in mind, we can learn to look at harmful behaviours through the lens of two questions:

- What is this person attempting to communicate through this behaviour?
- What is this person trying to gain or trying to ensure they don't lose?

The answer to the latter question could be something practical (money, a partner, a car) or intangible (status, power, self-esteem). Most of us want similar things in life — to be financially comfortable, to be loved, and to achieve meaningful things. Some of us have the capacities, skills, and power to achieve these in socially sanctioned ways; others default to unacceptable ways of grasping at these goals.

Another helpful action is recognising that most behaviours have more than one factor underpinning them. Some of these involve personality formation (yes, including narcissism), some are related to **psychological** functioning (being quick to anger, or unable to control emotion when it arises), yet others are **biological** (such as a strong compulsion to seek risk). There are also **social** factors either allowing or inhibiting certain behaviours. All of these factors interact. The biopsychosocial (biological-psychological-social)[4] model is commonly used to explain most types of mental health difficulties and is also very helpful in building an understanding of people who harm; I use this model in this chapter.

We often ignore the social facilitators of harm when considering other people's behaviour[5] and tend to focus on the psychological. However, the milieu one resides within — including one's peer group; prevailing social norms, including tacit or expressed approval of certain behaviours; the level of environmental containment provided; and the nature of one's relationships — impacts hugely on the behaviours a person uses. Most people have a range of behaviours available to them, and I am always amazed at how differently people can respond in certain situations, depending on what they hope to achieve and what the situation requires.

It is also helpful to remember that many forms of harm are not intentional. Most people don't deliberately set out to hurt someone else; it's far more common for people to justify their behaviours as 'right', or to deny harm, primarily to protect themselves from knowing what they're capable of. This does not absolve people, and the need for protection and intervention still stands. It can be psychologically useful, though, to remember that we all have this need to see ourselves as good and protect ourselves from knowing the ways in which we're not.

It might be helpful to explore the factors that lead to the perpetration of harm through a case study.

Adrian: a confluence of factors

Adrian was referred for treatment for stalking behaviours and intimate partner violence. He had repeatedly stalked multiple partners, quickly formed relationships, and entered turbulent commitments; most of his relationships were characterised by conflicts and misunderstanding. He often based his choices on physical attraction alone, paying no heed to deeper compatibility. He was quick to take offence, and was jealous, finding it difficult to trust in the fidelity of his partners. He had grown up seeing his parents engage in repeated extramarital affairs and said that this indelibly coloured his view of relationships. He was impulsive and irascible; he punched holes in the wall, and on one occasion, while intoxicated, he pushed his partner into a door, resulting in assault charges.

'I was never violent to her,' he said to me, somewhat defensively.

'Oh — pushing isn't violent?' I asked.

'You know what I mean … I didn't punch her,' he said.

Perhaps unsurprisingly, many of his relationships ended in turmoil, with his partners becoming tired of his demands on them, and his dogged suspicion and control. He became furious and pleading each time a partner left, determined to win them back. He engaged in a series of 'romantic gestures', such as placing gifts in their letterboxes, spraying his aftershave into their cars through open windows, and sending multiple text messages from a series of phone numbers. He believed that he was 'not being scary', and refused to recognise that his behaviour was stalking. In his mind, his ex-partners owed him another chance, and he was entitled to pursue them until they relented. Two of his ex-partners reported his behaviour to the police, and he was charged with stalking; he was incensed by this.

His most recent victim also approached the police for support after he pushed her, and an intervention order was placed against him. Intervention orders (sometimes called apprehended violence orders) are civil orders that restrain one individual from contacting, or harming, another individual. Breaches of these orders may result in criminal proceedings. While these orders can sometimes be helpful, they're often used indiscriminately (sometimes without the consent of the victim) by the police and courts in the absence of other management mechanisms, and are not always a helpful means of protection — sometimes even escalating risk. Adrian breached the order, scoffing at the 'piece of paper', and was quickly remanded in prison, eventually being sentenced to a community corrections order. He continued to express hostility and anger in his supervision meetings with his community corrections case manager, and they suggested a referral to my team to assess his risk of stalking (including his risk of engaging in physical violence again) and for treatment for the same. He firmly believed that he was not at fault, but that the police and the courts were 'out to get him' because he was a man.

'She hit me too,' he said. 'But no one cared about that because she's a woman. Everything is rigged against us [men].'

Biological factors

Temperament is a stable, biological construct, and we are all born with a certain type of temperament, strongly influenced by genetic components, in-utero environments, and prenatal development. Temperament is a key factor in whether a person will abuse or offend — though it isn't enough by itself to cause offending.

Adrian said he was a difficult baby and child. His mother's pregnancy was marked by several health issues and much marital stress. He was told that he was difficult to settle and that his parents found him hard to manage. He was colicky and cried a lot; his mother was often tired and left him to 'cry it out'. He remembered having frequent tantrums as a toddler and being overwhelmed when things were difficult at home, such as when his parents were fighting. He said that they fought a lot and were aggressive to each other. He didn't understand how he felt while watching them fight; he just remembered being 'furious' and lashing out. He repeatedly had scuffles with other children in primary school and was suspended on a few occasions. He had an irritable and unsettled temperament, prone to impulsivity and quick to anger. His temperament aligned with several developmental experiences (such as rejection from his peers) to form the basis for his personality. It is common for early childhood experiences to solidify temperamental traits.

Some people are easy babies — sleeping and eating well, growing, finding friends easily, and receiving excellent parenting because their parents are wellrested and find it easy to parent a placid and happy child. Other babies are irritable from the start, struggling to settle and soothe, needing much support, finding it hard to connect with peers. The parents of these children are often tired and irritable themselves, and struggle to be responsive and available to their children, perhaps setting up a family environment where there are clashes between the needs of child and parent, frequent smaller rejections, and a lack of support for the child with understanding the big emotions they may be experiencing. This is further compounded where parents have problems themselves, such as angry temperaments or issues with behaviours such as substance use.

This fit can be cataclysmic and can lead to a cascade of difficulties with social skills, schooling, work, emotional regulation, and anger management. The match between a child's temperament and that of their caregivers is very important. A child's temperament can mean that they are born with underlying levels of certain personality traits — such as proneness to impulsivity, reward sensitivity (i.e., how biologically rewarding they find stimulation), and dysregulated emotion — that mean that they simply cannot control their behaviour as well as children with more placid temperaments can. These traits involve essential biological differences in the tendency to detect, pursue, learn from, and derive pleasure from positive stimuli. Research has suggested that people with high reward sensitivity are more likely to seek pleasurable sensations like substance use; impulsive people find it difficult to inhibit action and to delay gratification.

Adrian had many of these traits, and he started drinking alcohol in early adolescence with older peers. He enjoyed alcohol and quickly became a regular drinker, using it to relax or manage distressing emotion. He found it hard to manage his anger, and tended to block out other emotions because they felt dangerous.

Children with temperaments like Adrian's may react with aggression or tantrums to smaller provocations, quickly becoming labelled a 'problem child' or 'disturbed', and perhaps becoming isolated at school, punished by teachers or ostracised by peers. Difficulties like ADHD diagnoses compound these troubles. All these problems eventually lead to a person perceiving the world in a certain way (e.g., 'People will abuse me', 'I am going to get in trouble anyway, so why bother?', 'I need to hit first to protect myself') and responding with harmful behaviours. The desire is rarely to inflict harm for the sake of enjoyment, but is often geared towards protecting oneself. It can also reflect beliefs about a 'dangerous' world and a desire for others to experience the pain that they feel. Adrian first started to fight with other children at school because they teased him about being bad at schoolwork. This eventually snowballed to him lashing out whenever he became angry.

Many people who impulsively commit interpersonal harms — such as violence in intimate relationships — have a background like that described above, including unsettled temperaments, high levels of impulsivity, longstanding difficulties regulating emotion, and a hostile attribution bias (the tendency to perceive provocation from relatively innocuous situations). Certain temperamental predispositions are likely to influence some of the more severe interpersonally harmful behaviours, such as sexual offending or intimate partner violence, in tandem with a range of other psychological factors and social influences.

Other biological factors include genetic predispositions to responding to the world in a certain way. Research has shown that those with a certain version of the gene responsible for transporting serotonin in the brain may be more susceptible to developing post-traumatic responses, depressive disorders, and alcoholism[6]. In-utero experiences also play a part — people with, for example, foetal alcohol spectrum disorders (FASD) find it very difficult to navigate the world, and are often only diagnosed if they have the facial features characteristic of the diagnosis, leaving other people perplexed about their often aggressive and impulsive behaviours.

Similarly, acquired brain injuries and intellectual disabilities are overrepresented in the prison population — possibly due to the impulsivity and behavioural instability that often occurs with prefrontal cortex injuries. The prefrontal cortex is responsible for all our higher-order cognitive capacities, including thinking abstractly, planning, organising, and inhibiting actions. Without it, we have all the emotional nous of a toddler — just in the larger body of an adult. Some of the most violent people I have worked with have severe acquired brain injuries.

Psychological factors

As we explored in chapters 2 and 3, survivors experience myriad difficulties with emotional regulation and the beliefs they have about the trauma, their selves, and the world. This is no different for people who perpetrate harm. Most forms of harm are underpinned by a range of psychological defences (denial and minimisation spring to mind), cognitive styles, personality traits, attitudes, and beliefs. Equally, difficulties recognising and managing emotion and problems with social skills are common.

Modelling: learnt behaviour

Adrian's parents were aggressive to each other, and while he was not consciously aware of forming belief structures based on the usefulness of violence to solve arguments, he tended to default to aggression and intimidation when threatened, or when someone disagreed with him. There are clear differences in the literature between anger (an emotion), aggression (hostile and intimidating behaviour), and violence (physical expressions of anger). People often conflate the three, but anger is a natural and protective emotion for all, and becomes problematic depending on how it is expressed. Occasionally, Adrian's anger emerged in violence, though only when he'd been drinking, so that that his usual inhibitions and controls were impaired. Alcohol use clearly did not *cause* his behaviours but it was the trigger that allowed his underlying attitudes and difficulties with emotion to be expressed.

When people cite alcohol and substance use as an explanation for their harmful behaviours, I usually remind them that many people consume alcohol and substances without becoming violent. I see substance use as the trigger that allows the gun to fire. However, even without the trigger, the gun is there, locked and loaded.

Adrian learnt early at school that bad behaviour would cause people to 'back off' and leave him alone. Being able to exert influence on the world around him was a potent reinforcer for the seven-year-old Adrian, and he continued these learned behaviours into adulthood, each episode — of using anger to change other people's behaviours or to get out of things he didn't want to do — reinforcing his aggression. However, Adrian as a fully grown man was much scarier than Adrian as a child for the people who encountered his aggressive behaviours.

People may use aggression, intimidation, or violence in one of two ways: to express themselves impulsively, without premeditation or forethought (expressive violence), or as a somewhat calculated way of achieving a certain aim (instrumental violence). For Adrian, both these mechanisms applied at different times. He had severe difficulties with managing emotion and very poor emotional recognition, and had not been supported to build emotional literacy as a child, instead being alternately rewarded and punished for anger but otherwise ignored.

Adrian was so enmeshed in defences of denial that he numbed most emotion (he said, for example, that he never felt sad) and was constantly tense and on high alert — sometimes bursting into anger as soon as he perceived that he was being provoked, or that a loss was threatened; at other times using intimidation in a more calculated way, to present as scary. He learnt this behaviour from his parents through observation and modelling — as most of us develop our templates and beliefs.

Sometimes extremely poor social skills can influence certain types of offending; for example, if people don't know how to communicate distress or ask to get their needs met ('I am sad, can you stay with me tonight?'), they may instead resort to aggression or withdrawal and passivity. Poor social abilities can make it much harder for people to make friends, retain jobs, and find healthy intimate partners — all of these difficulties can lead some people inexorably down a perpetration pathway, as they become further separated from what we generally consider qualities of a good life, and move further into harmful relationships and peer groups.

More insidiously, many child sex offenders demonstrate poor social skills and cannot form age-appropriate peer relationships. They either opportunistically harm children or engage in more planned and protracted attempts to sexually exploit or form 'relationships' with minors — with the term here reflecting the perpetrator's thoughts only. Children and adolescents cannot consent to sexual or intimate relationships with adults.

Some people who engage in child sex abuse (including viewing child-exploitation material) are extremely withdrawn and anxious when with same-aged peers, and default to only forming relationships with younger people to try to meet all their needs. I have worked with several people who have offended in this manner and desperately want to stop, but find it excruciatingly difficult to develop the skills needed to satisfy their needs in more appropriate ways. Of course, there are other offenders who are simply predatory.

Patterns of thinking and beliefs

I noticed that Adrian tended to minimise some of his behaviours ('It wasn't that bad'), rationalised others ('I only said that to stop her from yelling at me'), and denied some completely. He took little responsibility for his actions, relying instead on glib statements about the world being geared against men. He tended to deny the more shame-inducing aspects of his behaviours.

During treatment, he said he strongly believed that one must never hit a woman 'as they are weaker', a position he'd developed as a reaction to watching his father behave aggressively towards his mother. Interestingly, this in some ways negated the personhood of his partners, as he hid them beneath a veil of beliefs about women needing protection and being somehow less than men. There is an interesting dichotomy in my forensic work, where male offenders are aware that I know about the details of their violent or sexual offending (often directed at other women) but refuse to swear in front of me — believing that my delicate womanly ears will shrivel and fall off if I hear the word 'fuck'. Female offenders, on the other hand, often enjoy swearing in front of me and delight when I occasionally let something rude slip, as I am wont to do.

Adrian had a variety of scripts about the use of violence. 'Scripts' are cognitive structures and rules used as a way of understanding and responding to the world. A simple script that might lead to violence is 'If someone disrespects me, I hit them'. Those who inflict harm tend to have a range of these scripts around their behaviours.

Adrian did not have the psychological skills (emotional regulation, cognitive management) needed to align his behaviour with his beliefs about not hurting women, and he often acted in ways that went against them, quickly fleeing into the defences of denial ('I didn't do it') and intellectualisation ('I did it for x y or z reason') as a way of recovering his self-esteem and managing shame.

Treatment did not consist of smashing his defences or forcing him to confront what he had done (though I did at times challenge his views), but rather, lay in bolstering the part of him that didn't want to be aggressive and equipping him with alternative skills, including conflict resolution, emotional recognition and management, and communication. While some treatment programs geared towards helping people change their behaviours — notably the Men's Behaviour Change program in Victoria[7] (the primary treatment offered to men who perpetrate intimate partner violence) — use an antagonistic and confrontational style of treatment, people generally respond poorly to being publicly confronted and shamed. Treatment outcomes for this style of program are poor overall,[8] with limited effectiveness when looking at rates of reoffending, and many people's problematic attitudes and beliefs actually become more firmly embedded.

In general, I approach treatment with respect for the person and a goal to build up the positive before excavating the harmful. This doesn't mean that I don't challenge clients, but the challenging is built upon a bulwark of understanding and rapport. Not many of us will change our behaviours in an enduring way when shamed; instead, we learn to hide them. I use these general principles of behaviour change when working with offenders, too.

Attitudes

Often people who harm present with attitudes (i.e., a set of emotions, beliefs, and behaviours) that allow and enhance the offending. Common attitudes include entitlement ('I can do what I want, my needs are paramount'), minimisation of harm ('It was only a text message, it can't have been scary'), and a need to hold power over other people, regardless of the cost.

Entitlement is often overlooked in the public discourse on perpetration of harm, especially in intimate partner violence. People tend to focus on the 'role of women' and the 'power and control of men', with little thought given to how these norms play out in individual cases. I have found that most perpetrators do not present for treatment with explicit views about the subservience of women. Instead, their attitudes display a general entitlement, directed at everyone, with stronger expression of these attitudes directed at those closest to them (often, an intimate partner or children). Men are often socialised to have a greater sense of entitlement, easily taking up more space in the world without thought for those they share space with.

Perpetrators often hold certain views, sometimes subtle, about the differences between men and women, and direct blame towards women and the structures that support them. Sexualisation of women is common, with the clear view that the worth of a woman lies in her sexual attractiveness and her compliance — a view that underpins some sexual assaults. These views are entrenched in all domains of society, including legal systems (e.g., laws placing the onus of proving lack of sexual consent onto the victim), political systems, schools, institutions, the media, and families. They're often expressed by people (often, but not always men) who feel disenfranchised and powerless, or by those who have had a lot of power and find that power suddenly threatened. While gender-based attitudes underpin many harmful behaviours, they are never the sole and *inevitable* cause of these behaviours, otherwise every man would be violent towards female intimate partners, and there would be no violence (sexual or non-sexual) in same-sex intimate relationships.

Entitlement is the sense that one's needs are more important than those of other people. This attitude is implicitly encouraged and revered in our individualistic society, where we all become infuriated about our 'rights' — frequently forgetting that these rights are sustained by broader social obligations and responsibilities. We allow entitlement in certain culturally sanctioned ways, but react with horror when it crosses into the unacceptable. Entitlement underpins most harmful relational behaviours, including sexual violence towards adults and children, bullying, and intimate partner violence, and may sometimes reflect underlying tendencies towards narcissism.

Many of these attitudes are learned. Others are implicit in the social and familial structures people were raised within (including attitudes supporting the sexualisation and denigration of women), and yet others are developed as a defensive mechanism, such as a poorly treated child who decides that 'No one will ever hurt me again' and learns to become an intimidating bully themselves, in pursuit of safety.

Adrian had a clear sense of entitlement towards his partners. He also held beliefs like 'a shove isn't really violence', which contributed to his offences. Treatment involved making these unspoken attitudes explicit, so we could examine them and decide if they were helpful for him. As with most clients, I find that the quickest way to effect change is to try to get some 'buy-in', which means asking a client if their behaviour is working to get them what they want. The answer is usually no (if it was a yes, my forensic clients wouldn't be sitting in front of me), and noticing this fact allows me to stick my foot in the door and suggest that change might be useful.

Personality traits and emotional dyscontrol

Personality difficulties are common in people who perpetrate relational harm. Unless harm is being done in a calculated manner as an instrument (such as by those with psychopathic personality traits), it most often reflects a person's difficulties with managing themselves, delaying gratification, and inhibiting action (such as stopping the desire to lash out at someone who offends). Adrian had not developed these regulatory skills. These capacities are temperamentally driven, as we've discussed, but they can also be influenced and amended as we go through life, find positive role models, and gradually build understanding and self-regulation.

Personality structure is central to understanding perpetration. We all have a range of stable personality traits, the majority of these with genetic underpinnings, that are reinforced or brought to fruition by developmental experiences. The temperamentally shy child who experiences bullying at key developmental stages may withdraw from contact and become the avoidant adult. Similarly, the child with a very angry and unsettled temperament will likely become an aggressive adult when placed in a violent family living in significant chaos.

Our personality traits sit on a spectrum, from innocuous and adaptive to extremely problematic. Most of us will have some problematic personality characteristics — this is the nature of being human — and having insight into these traits is key to managing them. Personality traits manifest across a range of situations. They are part of our identity and form characteristic ways of responding — which is why we can never diagnose a personality disorder or problematic personality functioning based on one incident alone, no matter how heinous. We consider a range of personality traits when determining the causes of harm, including: hostility, a strong power orientation (i.e., a need to hold power); impulsivity; entitlement ('narcissism' is often used as shorthand); callousness (typically what we are referring to when we use the word 'psychopathy'); rigidity and propensities to hold absolute views (such that differing stances are intolerable); and tendencies towards severe emotional dysregulation (resulting in poor behavioural control when emotionally heightened).

Adrian did not have a diagnosable personality disorder, but he had clear traits of both borderline personality disorder and narcissistic personality disorder. He was entitled, struggled with experiencing rejection, responded with great emotional distress and anger when loss was threatened, and was very impulsive — all of which together predisposed him to behaving in harmful ways in his intimate relationships and close friendships. His narcissistic traits belonged to the subset of narcissism called fragile narcissism. We often distinguish between grandiose narcissism (i.e., people who genuinely believe that they are much more special than everyone else), and fragile narcissism (the same beliefs, but often developed as a compensation for a deep sense of inadequacy and self-loathing).

There is often nothing more emotionally dangerous than a fragile narcissist, as they throw all their psychological defences and behaviours at the purpose of maintaining their self-belief, regardless of what (or whom) they sacrifice in the process.

It is easy to miss fragile narcissists. Higher-functioning people will typically be able to manage these traits in their daily lives, only bursting into toxic action when they feel threatened. When I think of this, my mind is drawn to the image of a saltwater crocodile lying in wait, exploding into an attack only when their prey is close and most vulnerable. While saltwater crocodiles can sometimes be overcome, we are much better to avoid them, and keep a close eye on our surroundings when in croc-infested waters.

Another highly problematic cluster of personality traits is psychopathy, involving callousness, sensation-seeking, recklessness, impulsivity, grandiosity, superficial charm (yes — charm) and the inability to understand and feel common emotions. As I said earlier, there are very few true psychopaths (i.e., people who have the cognitive, emotional, *and* behavioural features of psychopathy), but many people who harm other people have some of these traits, usually clustered in the callous, unemotional, and reckless domains. If we can't feel what other people feel, we can't access the emotional cues we need to stop our behaviour (e.g., shame), or to plan our behaviours based not just on what we want and *our* rights, but also the rights and needs of other people.

I also want to tackle the concept of sociopathy here. This is a term that is commonly used, but is not derived from the mental health literature. It's a pop culture term used to refer to someone who we think has psychopathic or antisocial traits, or perhaps someone who simply behaves in ways we dislike. It's not a formal diagnosis and has little meaning.

Rigid views and obsessive traits are also highly challenging, as they often mean that people can't engage in basic social behaviours such as seeing something from another person's view or compromising. They will at times doggedly engage in very harmful behaviours (e.g., stalking someone they are angry with, or online trolling) because they can't view their behaviours objectively, consider the other person's stance, or take on corrective feedback.

The examples I have provided here tend towards the severe end of the spectrum of harm, but people who engage in other forms of interpersonally harmful behaviour demonstrate similar attitudes, personality traits, and beliefs. The mother who loses control and hits her child when her child is upset and screaming has difficulties with managing stress and emotion; just as the mother who might shake her child in a fit of rage, resulting in the child's death. The behaviour and emotions are similar in form; the differences are in the degree.

The manager who bullies may hold beliefs about hierarchy and power, and have a deeply hidden sense of inadequacy. They may instinctively respond to the capable employee by bullying and belittling, as a means of extinguishing a perceived threat.

An emotionally controlling partner may have a deep fear of rejection and loss and will cling desperately to avoid this loss, abusing their partner's rights and free will in the process. The violent partner may have similar fears, but their behaviours are exacerbated by learned behaviours around violence, a strong sense of entitlement, and a desire to inflict pain and have other people experience physically what they are feeling psychologically.

We all have the capacity to harm, given the right psychological underpinnings and circumstances.

Social factors: the catalyst

Most often when we think of people who harm, we blame the person. They are different to the rest of us; they are capable of something that we are not. Sometimes this is true, but most often, harm is underpinned by social circumstances; in fact, it can be explicitly encouraged by circumstances, facilitated by social factors, or discouraged by the society around us.

Consider the Catholic church, and the number of child sex predators who emerged from the archdiocese of Ballarat in Victoria from the 1960s to the 1990s. While many of these priests would have had paedophilic leanings, their behaviours were also facilitated by the social situation they were in: enforced celibacy within an environment that would protect them and excuse their behaviours, moving them along quietly as allegations emerged; unfettered access to children by virtue of running schools; a lack of child safety frameworks; a social milieu that revered the priesthood and had clear standards around shame, sin, and obedience; and colleagues who were engaging in the same behaviours and were thus invested in turning a blind eye and protecting each other. While some of these men would probably have engaged in child sex offences in other settings, their offence patterns would likely have been far less severe in environments with more emphasis on child safety, accountability, and victim empowerment.

When people use sexual violence in Victoria, they are placed on a sex offender register with limits on what they can do (e.g., child sex offenders are not allowed contact with those aged under 18 and cannot live within a certain radius of a school). Most jurisdictions around the world have similar legal structures, and when used well, these management tools can be very helpful in keeping people safe. A caveat here: publicly accessible sex offender registers do not reduce the risk that someone will reoffend[9] and may stop people from being able to reintegrate into society.

At present, absolute power is vested in certain organisations and people; legal structures are set up to allow and encourage victim-blaming; we enable the growth of rampant individualism and lack of regard for others through our focus on rights, and focus on building self-esteem without striving for a simultaneous increase in other-esteem. All these social factors contribute to the transmission of abuse. While we often rely on those in power to be ethical and to protect us, I tend to take the opposite view and approach people in positions of power, even those within certain professions, with more caution than I do your average, everyday person. Perhaps I am just cynical.

Other social factors include the relationships people build and the nature of these relationships (for instance, we know that stress and conflict within an intimate relationship influence the likelihood of violence,[10] as both partners struggle to manage emotion), how prosocial families and peer groups are (prosociality involves behaviours which promote social cohesion), availability of opportunities to harm, and factors protecting against the perpetration of harm (such as the careful eye of another adult in the household). Even simple factors — such as the amount of space available so that each individual in a family can have their own bedroom — may deter the opportunistic child sex offender, though this is unlikely to stop more motivated and planned offending.

Many harmful behaviours are stopped when people feel accountable to other people or beholden by social norms — so it's important to consider these factors and carefully build social systems that watch for and disallow harm.

Bringing it all together

I hope that this chapter has helped you build a better sense of the complexities that underlie abusive behaviours. These are complex, and fully understanding and formulating some of them requires many years of study and a good grasp of the forensic literature. Overall, though, if you can grasp the multifactorial nature of most harms, and are able to hold in mind the complexity of behaviour, you are well placed to start to understand abuse and harm.

When thinking of harmful behaviours, I like to expand on the questions I asked earlier (page 136) to guide my thinking. These questions might help you too:

- What is the harmful behaviour? Can I name it? What impacts does it have on people? Who does it impact?
- What does the person stand to gain from this behaviour?
- Is this behaviour part of a pattern? Can I see how it manifests across different situations (even at different degrees of severity)?
- Is there something in the person's personality structure that creates this behaviour? Are they often entitled? Callous? Angry? Demanding? Punishing?
- Is this person able to regulate and manage emotion? Do they have the social skills they need to communicate effectively and calmly?
- Does the person have any strong attitudes or beliefs that explain why they behave in this way?
- Which social structures implicitly allow or encourage this behaviour?
- Which social structures and changes to systems might stop this behaviour?

7

Identifying
Harmful People

Leonie had just turned 30 when she started seeing me. She was a social worker and worked in a hospital with children whose parents were suspected of abusing them. She was a central wheel in a complex system of child protection professionals, the medical system, the child themselves, and the family. Her role was to liaise with the family, which meant sensitively and carefully communicating concerns to them and managing the quagmire of feelings that arose — parents who became angered and sometimes violent, and children who wept and withdrew. She had exquisite communication skills. She paused often to consider her words and any subtle nuances she might be communicating. Many professionals in the health and social services fields have this skill of finely attuned communication, due to the nature of what they encounter, their overarching ethical position of 'do no harm', and their knowledge of the ways in which communication can go awry.

It seemed fair that Leonie held this stance at work, but I did note that bringing this self-censorship into her own relationships (including therapy) could lead to issues with self-expression and act as an obstacle to her building authentic and mutual relationships. I parked this thought to explore over time. As it turned out, this tendency was very informative when trying to understand what had happened to bring her to therapy.

Leonie had just had a relationship break down after finding out that her partner (Alan) had cheated on her, and she was struggling to come to terms with this. She'd invested a lot in the relationship, having assumed that by age 30, she would be in a long-term relationship and planning to have children. She was grieving, but she was also confused, and angry that she'd not noticed that Alan was cheating on her. It was interesting to note that she was angry with herself, and not with *him* — she explained that this was because at some stage of the relationship she had stopped expressing herself, and never disagreed with him or asked questions of him. She felt that if she had been able to express herself better, she would have found out about the infidelity earlier.

Over time, as her story unfolded, she told me how she'd met Alan on a dating app, and she was drawn to how confident and self-assured he was. Leonie was somewhat shy and diffident and enjoyed being in the presence of someone who embodied qualities she wished she had. She spoke of the first argument they'd had, when she'd disagreed with him about the importance of vaccinations (she worked in a hospital with very sick children and was pro-science and public health; he loudly believed that it was 'his body and his choice'). Alan shut down her dissent with 'Gee, as a social worker I thought you would be more open to views and opinions that don't align with yours.' When she tried to explain that her professional tolerances diverged from what she allowed in her personal life, he told her she was being hypocritical. As a reflective and self-aware person, she took his view on board.

However, he was unable to turn a similar lens on himself, and over time this dynamic led to a complete erasure of Leonie's views, as any dissent with him was shut down with statements like 'I thought you would be more accepting'. As she withdrew into herself, she found that he became more controlling and critical in his views about how she should think, feel, or behave. Each time she tried to speak up, it ended in an argument. Alan often told her that her interpretations of events and memories were wrong, leaving her confused and worried about her own thoughts and feelings. He was never physically violent to her, but she reflected that this was 'almost worse … at least if he had hit me, I would have been able to see it for what it was and end it'.

Finding out that Alan had cheated on her for most of their relationship was the catalyst for the end of the relationship. Leonie felt intense relief but was also angered, and over time, her anger shifted to be directed at him. We worked out that there really are no conclusive ways of establishing if a partner is cheating on us without breaching boundaries ourselves, and that good relationships require a solid measure of trust.

We also worked out that her former partner had never been trustworthy. He was self-absorbed and highly critical of Leonie, he breached her boundaries over time, was unable to take responsibility for his own actions and views, and his confidence was really just thinly veiled ignorance and self-centredness. The signs of bad behaviour were subtle and were present in the *psychological* dynamics of the relationship rather than in anything overt he did.

Before I started writing this chapter, I reflected on the cognitive shortcuts I use to identify people who might be harmful. Most of my knowledge in this area is drawn from my work in the forensic field, where people present with entrenched and known histories of perpetrating harm and abuse. This makes it difficult to pick out specific factors which *may* signal harm, as I already know the outcome for all my forensic clients. It's been tricky to condense my clinical radar and forensic knowledge into a set of guidelines to help us navigate interactions with people who harm, largely because the signs are often relatively ambiguous and subtle.

Ultimately, I've focused on exploring those behaviours we commonly notice and excuse away, or those that we see but think are inconsequential. Many of the harm-signalling behaviours I describe will be familiar; I suspect that most people instinctively know *how* to recognise those who might harm us, but have a range of defences, justifications, and blind spots that mean we don't *want* to recognise them. Perhaps we want love so badly that we refuse to see the abusive partner; maybe we have a deep-seated sense of anxiety and inferiority, and the ferocious bully feeds right into these vulnerabilities, stopping us from noticing that they are a bully.

In many ways, this chapter is likely to tell you what you already know but will also explain *why* your intuitive knowing might be correct. Sometimes we just need permission to see what is in front of us so we can act protectively; consider this permission given.

When we speak about those who may harm us, we often focus on the stranger in the bushes — the attacker who will ambush us in the dark of the night, or the rapist who will break into our house — instead of casting our eyes over the cast of characters in our lives: the family members, the friends, the colleagues, managers, dates, acquaintances. Most relational abuses are perpetrated by those closest to us.

In Australia, the Australian Bureau of Statistics[1] says that 17 per cent of women (1.6 million) and 4.3 per cent of men (385,000) have experienced sexual assault since age 15, usually by someone known to them. Eleven per cent of women (1 million) and 4.6 per cent of men (412,000) experienced childhood sexual abuse, usually by a known person outside the biological family, such as a stepparent. The Australian Institute of Health and Welfare[2] found that in 2014–15, on average, almost eight women and two men were hospitalised each day after being assaulted by their spouse or partner. Almost one in four (23 per cent) women and one in six (16 per cent) men have experienced emotional abuse from a current or previous partner since the age of 15. Between 2012 and 2014, one woman a week and one man a month were killed as a result of violence perpetrated by a current or previous partner.[3]

All intimate partner violence, child neglect, intra-familial child physical abuse, and bullying, by definition, are perpetrated by people well known to the victims. Instead of spending too much time considering stranger danger and planning ways to evade this, we are far better served by looking at our own behaviours (if people are most often being harmed in relationships, then many of us are, necessarily, doing the harming), considering ways to identify those who are truly harmful, developing good boundaries, learning how to decrease the likelihood that we will harm, and building and using structures that protect everyone.

Not every difficult or aversive behaviour is harmful. Most of us will occasionally behave with defensiveness, rudeness, or frustration, though hopefully this does not become a pattern, or involve aggression, violence, intimidation, or any form of coercion. It is important to understand and recognise that most people will behave in a manner that hurts someone else on occasion — this does not make everyone harmful and does not mean that we must protect ourselves from every type of hurt, or address and challenge every behaviour that mildly offends us. Sometimes the things that offend us speak more to our sensitivities than to the intentions or psyches of the people doing the offending.

It's likewise essential to differentiate between those who are largely harmless but may respond or act in ways that sometimes displease others, and those who are actively harmful and abusive, whether intentionally or otherwise. It's also helpful to match our responses to the behaviour, and to reserve our strongest responses for the largest harms, such as sexual assault, severe emotional abuse, or violence. Often, psychologically abusive behaviours are subtler and can initially go unnoticed by victims and other people — such as the behaviours Alan (Leonie's partner) engaged in — but many explicitly harmful behaviours often occur after a period of slow escalation. Most physically harmful behaviours are also accompanied by psychologically abusive behaviours, and it is these behaviours that can act as warning beacons for us. These psychologically abusive behaviours are what we sometimes call coercive control. When I work with victims of abuse, common questions arise. Some of these are:

> Did I miss any red flags?
> Why did I miss those red flags?
> What could I have done to stop this?

This chapter seeks to answer some of these questions and aims to help people identify those who demonstrate *patterns* of coercive and harmful behaviour within interpersonal relationships, and to build skills in managing these people. By noticing harmful behaviours before they escalate too far, we can protect ourselves before we experience significant psychological damage. The question of stopping behaviour is difficult, as abuse is based on the perpetrator's choices, not the victim's. However, sometimes learning to notice signs of abuse means we can protect ourselves (and I discuss how later in this chapter), though this is a big task at times, and can seem hard or impossible.

I like to differentiate between those who perpetrate harm for *predatory* reasons and deliberately choose to override the rights and safety of others for personal gratification (child sex abuse is often an example of this); those who harm in an *uncontrolled* manner (i.e., those who don't intend to hurt other people but find it difficult to control their behaviours in certain situations, such as the parent who hits their child in a fit of rage); and those who harm *unconsciously*. The latter are likely to be blind to their behaviours and impacts on other people and may be driven by a sense of deep moral righteousness ('I'm doing this for a valid and virtuous reason') or fragile narcissism ('How dare you call me selfish, I will destroy you'). People who embark on campaigns of online harassment and trolling, including doxxing, sometimes belong to the latter group, especially if they begin this behaviour in pursuit of a worthy cause (e.g., mounting protracted campaigns against people they see as predatory). Doxxing involves searching for and publishing private and identifying information about someone on the internet, typically with malicious intent, and is illegal in most jurisdictions.

There is usually some interplay between these motivations, and people can cause severe harm regardless of their motivations. I often think of a family violence offender I once worked with. He had multiple victims, one of whom eventually killed herself. While he did not contribute directly to her death, it's likely that the turmoil of the relationship and subsequent harassment had affected her already turbulent mental state. The harm caused to her was severe, though his behaviours were uncontrolled and unconscious, not deliberately predatory, and he had no way of predicting the outcome. People are more fragile than we realise, and smaller harms can also be what pushes someone past the point of no return.

As we consider ways of identifying and managing those who harm, we must also be aware that we will never be able to identify every person with harmful behaviours — some people are skilled at presenting a particular front. However, as I said in the last chapter, sometimes we're best placed to avoid a crocodile attack by understanding their behaviours, territories, and modus operandi, though we hope that systems of crocodile management mean we are never subject to an attack. Similarly, we can seek to understand people who demonstrate harmful behaviours and find ways to separate ourselves from them and manage them, while still fundamentally relying on the structures around us to keep us safe.

Most abusive behaviours occur in *secrecy* and always within structures that allow this. Many people who engage in abusive behaviours understand that they are harmful and go against general societal norms, so they enact these behaviours in private, usually when only the victim is present. A child sex offender will try to separate the victim from other children or family; an abusive partner will only scream and yell inside the home; an abusive parent will say something like 'don't wash your dirty linen in public', as a way of dissuading a child from talking to others; a bullying manager will save the worst of their behaviours for behind a closed door. Sometimes behaviours will escalate slowly, as someone finds reinforcement for their actions or becomes more brazen as they feel more certain that they will not be caught or punished. Secrecy is essential and makes it difficult for a victim to identify that these behaviours are occurring and to seek support. People who engage in abusive acts often demonstrate situation- and context-dependent behaviours, so that people who are *not* being victimised by them will see very different behaviours.

One of the most difficult experiences for trauma victims is statements by other people like, 'But s/he is so nice!' Some clients have said that this makes them feel 'crazy' as they quickly start to doubt their own perceptions. I usually remind these clients that we can all be nice when we choose, and that even true psychopaths can present as some of the nicest people — when they want something from you. Niceness is wholly inadequate as a behavioural barometer and often merely means that a person can maintain a social façade and be charming, engages in impression management (i.e., carefully tailors how they present themselves), or has poor boundaries and very passive communication styles — effectively being seen as 'nice' because they never confront people and never say no, and other people can override and exploit this passivity.

Our perception of someone could be very different to another person's experience of them, and a range of behaviours could sit under an impression of charm and care. People are not monsters and it is entirely possible for someone to be genuinely kind in one situation and harmful in another.

When trying to identify harmful behaviours, I focus on a few key principles.

Past behaviour is the best predictor of future behaviour

This is a core forensic psychological maxim, and we use it when understanding all kinds of harmful behaviours and when planning for risk scenarios (i.e., trying to predict the highest-risk situations for perpetration of harm).

Identifying harmful people involves a careful assessment of someone's behaviour over time. We often struggle to accurately assess motivations and thoughts/feelings; people may say one thing and do another, often with the best intentions and poor follow-through. It is important to allow enough time for patterns to emerge. We are all on our best behaviour at the beginning of a relationship — whether a new friendship, a new job, or an intimate relationship. Allowing relationships to build slowly allows us to assess the safety of people before we are enmeshed too deep within a relationship. This is, at its simplest, structural — it is easier to exit a relationship in which someone belittles us when we don't live with them and share a lease, and much easier to end a relationship before we have a shared mortgage and children.

Looking carefully at a person's behaviour over time and across a range of settings should show us how they will treat us. It's important to watch how someone behaves towards those who have less power than they do, and how they behave when a limit is set or a boundary established. People are often nice when they are allowed to do as they wish, only demonstrating patterns of harmful behaviour when they perceive a challenge or a threat to their power.

The person who was rude to the waiter and dismissive of and furious at their ex-partner? Unlikely to treat new partners with care and consideration. Someone who tries to insist that you have sex with them though you've said that you don't want sex, and speaks vindictively about gender equity and feminism? This behaviour is likely learned, part of a pattern, and reeks of entitlement and dismissal of your needs. It will not easily change. The manager who comes with a reputation for bullying or harassing staff? Be wary. Someone who is known for punching holes in the wall when angry? They are unlikely to respond to conflict with you with consideration and good communication.

My general rule is that if something is done *around* me, it could be done *to* me.

Our tendency might be to excuse certain behaviours, or to believe that they will not happen to us because we can 'fix' someone. This is especially likely if we have histories of relational traumas ourselves and internalised negative beliefs about our own worth, or if certain types of behaviours were permissible in our families. This is often the crux of repeated traumas: normalisation of subtle harmful behaviours such that someone struggles to recognise the signs that another person may be problematic until the behaviours have progressed to a point where they can no longer be denied. We might hold out hope that we can change someone if we care enough for them, but this is unlikely to be true. Behavioural change requires motivation, insight, time, and effort. Love and care alone are manifestly inadequate.

Identifying harm also involves developing the capacity to distinguish between helpful and harmful relationships. This capacity is often greatly impaired in people who have experienced interpersonal trauma for a few reasons: abusive behaviours were often normalised and explained away; the survivor's experiences were scoffed at, leading them to distrust their own instincts; and people will try to compensate, wanting to please others, drowning out the inner voice of caution. Having a good understanding of these factors helps to assess the psychological safety of other people. I often use a simple traffic light flag system with clients: safe (green), unsafe (red), and pause-to-think (orange) relationships, behaviours, and interactions. This allows them to evaluate relationships and interactions through the lenses of relational health and psychological safety.

When considering red flag behaviours, I look for known histories of harmful behaviour and difficulties with self-regulation, such as people who struggle to manage and express emotion in safe and healthy ways, instead behaving in explosive or hurtful ways. I notice behaviours such as boundary pushing, insistence that someone is always correct in their views, and difficulties with recognising and accepting dissent.

I look for issues of control — someone telling a partner who to see, what to wear, or where to go, especially if this extends beyond attempting to keep someone safe (i.e., a partner telling you that you cannot drive when intoxicated is not controlling). 'Control' comes up in colloquial discourses about violence in relationships, and usually describes attempts to get one's relational needs met by reducing the other party's agency and capacity to leave the relationship. Adult relationships should never be based on one person having more control than the other, and each person should be free to express their views and needs, and to have a level of autonomy and privacy.

The crux of coercive control or emotional abuse is one person's efforts to keep the other trapped in the relationship. This may involve things like isolating someone and controlling where they go, or perhaps putting them down so often that their self-esteem crashes. Coercive control is not often a planned strategy (i.e., the perpetrator has not deliberately mapped out what they will do and *why*), but is a very problematic pattern that often develops out of the perpetrator's personality traits (such as impulsivity, jealousy, and emotionality), attitudes, communication patterns, and poor emotional and self-management skills.

One litmus test of harm is to notice how someone responds when told 'no'. It's easy to be pleasant and polite while interactions are positive and friendly; it's in watching someone address a 'no', or a 'stop now', that we can determine how respectful they're likely to be.

Do they try to talk us out of it? Push us to change our mind? Rationalise their behaviour? Become angry at us? These are all red flags.

Some people are inconsistent in their behaviours and move between being loving and being harmful. This is an incredibly problematic cycle that underpins much intimate partner violence and coercive control. It keeps a victim desperately seeking 'forgiveness' and reparation, leaving the perpetrator with the power to grant or withhold forgiveness and care. This is often colloquially called a 'trauma bond', and the victim can experience powerful reinforcement through occasional love and care, often trying to work out what they can do to make a perpetrator treat them well again.

Being overly pushy or forceful with communication can constitute a red flag, as can strong attempts to move a connection forward quickly or to have needs met, disrespecting the needs of other people in the process. When working with stalkers, I have noticed that their initial approaches while forming relationships are marked by a certain forcefulness and lack of appropriate pacing. This reflects a great desire to form relationships quickly and can result in intense emotional fluctuations when these relationships are threatened.

Other communication-based red flags include refusal to listen to alternative views and attempts to make someone second-guess their own views and experiences, much as Leonie's partner did. It is respectful to listen to how other people perceive something, even if we then want to offer a counterview. Shutting someone down with a 'No, that's not how it was', or 'You are overreacting', points to the possibility of ongoing conflict. Equally, the refusal to acknowledge that someone else could have a different and valid view of an interaction can be harmful, especially if this is underpinned by low self-awareness and insight. We often (incorrectly) use the term 'gaslighting' to attack someone for expressing a different view to us, and this is abusive behaviour itself. Similarly, the words 'manipulation', 'toxic', and 'triggering' are sometimes used to shut down people's views.

Boundary breaches

As Leonie and I continued to work together, we explored some of her other relationships. She dated a man in her early 20s who told her about a time he became intoxicated, very angry, and kicked his ex-girlfriend's car, leaving a dent. She said that he wanted sex early one morning, on a day when she had an exam and was not interested in sex. She said no, but he coaxed, implored, and begged; she remained firm. He eventually got up sulkily and said he was going to leave if she didn't have sex with him. 'Fine,' she said, 'you know you can't coerce me into sex — no means no.'

'I wasn't even trying, coercing you wouldn't work anyway.' Leonie said that she will always remember this statement — she took the subtext to mean: 'I would try to coerce you if I thought you would give in'. Later that weekend, he had a furious tantrum about how she used the phrasing 'no means no', because he was 'not a rapist'. He was not a rapist, but of course, consent is not true consent if it is coerced. This appears to be a surprisingly difficult concept for many men. Australia's National Research Organisation for Women's Safety Limited (ANROWS) conducted a number of surveys into attitudes towards sexual consent[4] and found very poor knowledge about consent among young Australians, with 1 in 7 Australians believing that a man is entitled to force sex if a woman initiates it, but then changes her mind. A quarter of young men think it's flattering for a woman to be pursued, even if she has said no (FYI, just to make it *very* clear —

this is called stalking, and once sexual consent is withdrawn, forcing sex is sexual assault or rape).

Once this man broke up with Leonie a few months later, she started seeing someone else. This man told her that one of the first things he'd noticed about her was how still she sat. She remembered that she'd noticed him watching her and had been sitting still because she was uncomfortable with his attention and being stared at in a public place. What does it say about a person, that stillness should be the thing they are drawn to — the passivity and prey-freeze responses produced by discomfort or perception of danger?

This man was two hours late to their second date. One night, when they were having sex, he was extremely rough, and she was in pain. 'Stop,' she said, pushing at him. He didn't. That relationship didn't last; it wasn't long before it imploded in a flurry of furious text messages from him when he perceived that she had slighted him. While it was painful at the time, she was grateful that it ended when it did. She also said that perhaps having these poor experiences meant that she allowed the relationship with Alan to continue for longer. 'At least he never forced me to have sex,' she said.

I offer these stories here to share how small the initial inklings of harm can be. What someone says about an ex-partner, how respectful they are of someone else's time, how they manage anger, what they notice and like about us, whether they consider our comfort, how they respond when we say no or ask them to stop. From these observations, we build our ideas of people.

Boundaries are frequently discussed and poorly understood, but they're essential for maintaining good mental health and a key part of learning to identify people who might be harmful. Boundaries are also one of the hardest concepts for trauma survivors to understand and practise, because of the boundary breaches that were often modelled and encouraged.

At their most basic, boundaries are a recognition of opportunity costs and the idea that we have limited resources and need to conserve those resources so we can best do what we need to do. They're a key part of psychological wellbeing, and involve physical, emotional, mental, financial, and time-based limits. We set them for ourselves and for others. We all have different boundaries; we may have different boundaries for different people, based on levels of closeness and social roles. The boundaries I hold for acquaintances, for example, are very different, and much firmer, than those I hold for my closest people.

People who abuse other people are fundamentally crossing boundaries, and these boundary-crossing behaviours may be subtle at first. They could come as explicit attempts to ignore your boundaries, or as the perpetrator crossing the boundaries of *their* role — such as a counsellor becoming a client's friend, or starting to touch them. Most of these behaviours will initially be relatively subtle; they may feel pleasant and make a client feel 'special'. A slippery-slope effect[5] has been noted with health practitioners who are found guilty of serious violations of their professional code (such as having sex with a client) — indicating that boundary breaches and role transgressions commence in minor ways, and then escalate. Boundary breaches are likely to be present in most types of abuse, not just that enacted by misbehaving professionals.

In general, I am suspicious of those who breach the core boundaries of their roles, even if it's done to benefit someone else. Professional boundaries exist to protect clients and have been well considered over time. Violating these boundaries is a deliberate decision to discount the structures that keep us all safe; sometimes, it's indicative of a practitioner's own psychological functioning and their need to be 'special' or different. Even boundary breaches that seem to benefit clients may be harmful, as they set up expectations that often cannot be maintained. It is normal for some boundaries in any relationship to fluctuate a little, and for boundaries to be flexible based on need, but the core role boundaries should always remain. I will sometimes, after careful consideration, relax my personal boundaries around phone contact and contact between sessions for clients who need this, but there are other boundaries — such as no physical, social, or sexual contact with a client — that will remain sacrosanct.

Good boundaries are the crux of relational safety. Simple violations such as still receiving messages from someone when we've asked them to stop may feel inconsequential, but the underlying subtext with these actions is 'My needs are more important than yours, and I don't respect what you have said'. People who have very poor boundaries themselves are more likely to override other people's — it's hard to maintain for others that which we do not see for ourselves — but most people with poor boundaries will still be respectful of other people's boundaries once they have been explicitly stated. The red flag of harm resides in people pushing or ignoring reasonable, *stated* boundaries. Someone who repeatedly does so is demonstrating entitlement, lack of regard for our views, and disrespect.

Secretive behaviours and structures

As explored earlier, relational traumas and abuses most often occur in secrecy. Very little abuse occurs in the broad light of (metaphorical) day, and the worst behaviours are usually reserved for situations where the person perpetrating harm and the victim find themselves alone.

While we are undoubtedly going to be alone with various people over the course of our lives, it's helpful to notice if someone is attempting to create more secrecy or privacy than the situation warrants. Examples include someone repeatedly offering to care for a child away from the family home, or an employee being rostered on alone with a manager who has already been sexually suggestive. Deliberate attempts to create secrecy and separate someone more vulnerable from other people, especially when accompanied by boundary-crossing behaviours, are red flags.

When considering harm, it is also essential to consider the structures within which harm occurs. Structures that involve a differential in power and implicit expectations of obedience create situations ripe for perpetration of harm — such as the command-and-control structures used in organisations like defence and police forces. Expectations of obedience and compliance ensure that people feel they must obey those in authority, and don't feel empowered to speak up about what they experience and witness — effectively ensuring that perpetrators are able to remain hidden. It's common for those who *do* speak up to be vilified and punished, which acts as a deterrent for other people.

Within Australia, we have had, to date, several media exposés about the Australian Defence Force and the severe bullying and repeated sexual harassment/assaults that have occurred within its ranks, revealing the danger of an uninformed culture with norms around certain forms of masculinity, and the expectation of stoic and indifferent compliance. We've seen similar incidents within prisons, where people who speak up are often called 'lags' or 'dogs', and are ostracised and bullied by their peers, usually until they leave. Religious organisations are similar. I find that people who think they have some form of religious or spiritual mandate can believe they are above the law of the land. This is very harmful, as it means they have no sense of accountability and effectively do whatever they want because they rationalise that it is justified by their god. Religion is a startlingly convenient cover for many abusive people.

Situations that involve significant power differentials between people create conditions where harm may occur. Many professions have power imbalances inherent within their structures — including medicine, law, psychology, psychiatry, law enforcement and the clergy — and no system, institution, or profession is above containing individuals who are drawn to it precisely *for* this power differential and the opportunity to exert influence over other people. Working within a system that privileges some views and experiences, and allows individuals to believe that they're always correct or are the ultimate arbiter of justice, means that they may develop a god-complex of sorts and engage in unpleasant behaviours when their power is threatened or when someone disagrees with them.

The role of psychological coercion

Most physical abuse within relationships is underpinned by slowly escalating patterns of psychological abuse and coercion (though these patterns of abuse or coercive control can exist without physical harm, and may be just as damaging). The typical early warning signs of abuse can be subtle, but still manipulative, coercive behaviours. The concept of emotional 'manipulation' is charged, and is often levelled at another person with great anger and blame, even in the forensic settings I work in. Patients are seen as 'manipulative' and 'splitting staff'. In reality, all of us attempt to influence the behaviour of other people to get our needs met, and if given a chance, we would all align ourselves with people who are kind to us and seek them out for interactions, ignoring those who are unpleasant. We all manipulate people daily, in different ways.

Manipulation can be largely defined as the behaviours someone uses that are designed (perhaps unconsciously) to help them satisfy their needs — for example, the much maligned 'gaslighting'. Gaslighting is an umbrella term derived from the 1944 film *Gaslight*, where a husband convinces his wife that she is going crazy by subtly dimming their gas-fuelled lights each day and telling her she's hallucinating. Initially, gaslighting referred to a pattern of behaviour, usually intentional, designed to make someone question their own reality, memories, or experiences. At its most basic, it involves trivialising and dismissing the experiences of another, and punishing them for voicing their experiences. Over time, concept creep has meant that we now misidentify many behaviours as gaslighting, including simple disagreement between parties about memories or experiences. None of us are going to experience or remember things in exactly the same way.

Coercion and manipulation are rarely deliberate, conscious strategies designed to make a victim feel 'crazy'. Instead, they're usually focused on increasing victim access (i.e., people are more likely to spend time with someone once they've undergone a grooming process), bolstering the perpetrator's views of themselves (i.e., if someone acknowledged that their behaviours were harmful, they would have to amend their behaviours or change their positive views of themselves), or getting their needs met, such as ensuring that a victim remains compliant. Keeping this in mind means your attention can shift from trying to desperately understand *why* someone is doing something to noting and addressing the behaviours. Coercive behaviours are quite simple — they exist because of the perpetrator's own psychological defences, attitudes, and skills deficits, their need to maintain positive views of themselves, and to ensure victims remain compliant and in their influence. These behaviours can be very subtle, such as putting someone down, or more obvious, such as overt threats.

When considering emotionally coercive behaviours, I encourage people to look for *patterns of behaviour* and at whether or not people can recognise and amend their behaviours. Isolated instances of bad behaviours are common — we've all lashed out in anger or blamed someone else when we've felt defensive — but they become problematic when they occur repeatedly over time, are accompanied by a lack of insight, there are no attempts to make reparation, and/ or they're accompanied by physical abuse. Emotionally coercive behaviours can occur in all relationships, though we most often talk about them in intimate relationships. The Australian Bureau of Statistics recently released a report stating that 23 per cent of women and 16 per cent of men have experienced emotional abuse by a partner since the age of 16.[6] Harmful behaviours in relationships are unfortunately very common.

Emotionally coercive behaviours are damaging, regardless of their function or the setting within which they occur. I have worked with a number of people who have experienced coercion in intimate relationships, without physical abuse. For many of them, it was harder to recognise and respond to this behaviour, as it was not as obvious as physical abuse. It slowly escalated over time, from subtle disapproving comments about their friends to strong elements of control.

The most common examples of psychologically coercive behaviours include:

- Frequently belittling someone, name-calling, frequent teasing (teasing can be innocent and fun, but not when underpinned by sarcasm and malice), or dismissing feelings.
- Stepping outside role boundaries and seeking secrecy around these behaviours.
- Asking people to keep harmful secrets (e.g., asking a child to not divulge violence within the home to people at school).
- Outright denial that certain events occurred.
- Threatening social disapproval or isolation if certain 'secrets' are revealed.
- Threatening to 'expose' someone if they do not comply (such as occurs with image-based abuse).
- Behaviours designed to isolate someone from other people or to control their actions, such as parents not allowing children to have friends.
- Explicit threats to harm the victim, or those close to the victim, if secrets are revealed (sometimes used by perpetrators of child sex abuse).

- Making someone feel 'special' or signalling that a relationship is closer than it is (often utilised by child sex abusers).
- Threatened withdrawal of care or love if someone does not comply.

Relationships characterised by these behaviours are not safe or psychologically healthy, even without any form of physical harm occurring.

Psychological abuse in organisations

Abusive behaviours also happen in other structures, such as at work. Workplace bullying has gained a lot of attention because of the huge impacts it can have on people's mental health. Bullying behaviours are a form of abuse. It can be difficult to recognise bullying, in part because it's such an umbrella term and encompasses a variety of behaviours. Legally, the definition is very strict and it's often hard for behaviours to meet this threshold. The root of bullying is a repeated pattern of behaviours that intimidate, harass, or denigrate another person. Bullying often involves a use of power, and it is difficult (but not impossible) for someone to bully an individual who has some form of power over them. By its very definition, bullying is inflicted on the disempowered.

Sometimes, bullying is done by those who have no experience with managing staff, and either no awareness of power dynamics or utter disregard for them. Sometimes, it's entirely unintentional, and the bully would be horrified to know that their behaviour could be construed that way. People often become managers when they've stuck around for long enough in the same profession, and they may have no training in the interpersonal skills needed or in the competencies required to manage different personalities and balance competing needs. It isn't hard not to bully, but it requires a person to understand power, their own behaviour (and how they're perceived), and the ability to communicate sensitively and efficiently, even if providing negative feedback.

Like many Australians, I have been bullied at work myself. I once had a manager who was very nice at first and seemed to have close relationships with her staff. A few months into the job, she started to provide me with performance feedback in an aggressive manner. She berated me for small mistakes, on one occasion calling me into her office, backing me into a corner, and pointing at me, her face furious and red. She was a statuesque woman, with much more power than I had, so this felt threatening and terrifying. I began to feel a sense of dread and anxiety when going in to work, and felt like I had to cover up anything that went wrong and work harder. She also made several statements that made me feel as if other people at work were watching me and questioning my commitment and competence. I was always anxious, and always on edge. The more anxious I became, the more mistakes I made.

Eventually, I realised that a couple of colleagues also looked miserable, and we started talking about work. I discovered that they had been subject to the same behaviours I had, and that most of us in the team had cried at work at some point. Other people had begun to notice our manager's behaviours, because we had changed location and were less isolated, and the solace of heads popping up over cubicles and a sympathetic glance helped to validate our experiences. Unfortunately, bad behaviour begets bad behaviour, and a small number of people who worked closely with her started engaging in similar behaviours. Eventually, we left, in dribs and drabs over months, most of us carrying some psychological scarring. We spoke about it later — our confusion when these behaviours started to occur, the juxtaposition of her smiling exterior and the pointed anger we saw, her excellent treatment of a handful of staff members and the denigration of others, the self-blame, the slow escalation of behaviour, and some of the odd things she said to us, which made us question our own experiences and thoughts. Her behaviour was psychologically damaging for many of us. As a manager, she was entitled to provide feedback, but she was not entitled to her unrealistic expectations, and nor was she entitled to provide feedback in the aggressive manner she chose — these subtle differences moved her behaviour from acceptable to psychologically unsafe.

None of these behaviours were overt, and they weren't at the pointy end of bullying I've heard about from clients — some of whom have been harassed, teased, ostracised, repeatedly rostered on for shifts they did not want, discriminated against, sexually harassed, or shouted at. Nevertheless, they were enough to destroy my confidence for months.

Bullying can be a difficult behaviour to understand, and while its motivations are likely to be manifold, they will probably fit within the conceptions I have provided elsewhere. The behaviour will most often serve to support the bully with gaining something tangible (a promotion, more work) or intangible (power, self-esteem), or with protecting against some form of loss (status, financial losses). We have complex relationships with work, and, in our modern capitalist societies, it consumes a large part of our identity, rendering our behaviours even more complex as we strive to make a mark, feel seen and heard, or protect our territory. We're forced into artificial groups at work by being placed in teams, and spend large amounts of time with people unrelated and unknown to us, who may be entirely unlike us in psychological make-up. It's easy for conflict to arise, and for power to be abused when resolving these problems. Some people are just difficult — they have problematic ways of expression and communication, and these appear at work just as they would in the person's own home and friendships, though those who encounter them at work often have more limited choice or power.

In practice

If you are feeling overwhelmed by the information in this chapter, it may be helpful to think about how we can use it in practice. I use these principles in different ways in my own life, focused on safety and respect for all.

I pace the development of new friendships and relationships. I notice how people respond to a no and respect other people's nos. I have boundaries with friends, family, and clients. I very quickly block people on my public-facing social media accounts if they are rude (disagreement is fine, attacks are not). I don't read the comments section.

I notice if people have specific role or gender expectations of me. As an example, in a dating context, I never swipe right on someone who talks about wanting a 'lady', or someone 'feminine' (this points to specific gendered expectations). I observe how people approach sexual consent with me — do they ask, simply assume, or even consider the matter as important? If someone assumes consent or tries to engage in sexual acts without some form of question or non-verbal gesture, I don't see that person again. I now won't see someone again if they are pushy about sex once I've said no (though I did make this mistake when I was younger). I seek consent before engaging in sexual contact myself ('Is this okay?', 'Do you like this?'). While people don't often talk about women seeking consent (and very few women perpetrate sexual harm), I try to be the change I want to see in the world, which means asking permission.

I watch how people treat other people. I notice if people tend to have lots of conflict with others in their life, hold the victim role, and have little awareness of their own behaviours. I watch if people are really nice to other people, but then cut them down privately later. We all gossip or complain at times, and, as always, this is about whether this behaviour is a pattern.

I ask workplaces questions about issues like culture, bullying and harassment. I am a member of the union. I know my rights and responsibilities under my contract and the award under which I am employed. I treat other people at work respectfully and think carefully about power differentials, both with clients and colleagues. I am honest and firm, but also try hard to be compassionate. I ask to be paid for most of the work I do. If I have an issue with someone at work or elsewhere, I try to talk to them about it directly first. I made a decision early in my career that I won't work with people once they have been abusive, threatening, or aggressive to me — no, not even therapy clients.

Many people will read this list and say 'geez, she's a bit demanding and difficult' — these words (as well as my other favourite words, 'angry', 'bossy', and 'bitchy') are so often levied against women (especially women of colour) who are strong and know what they want. These guidelines have filtered out maybe 5 per cent of my contacts (the rest are incredible people, and have allowed me to live a very safe, fulfilling, and drama-free life).

Identifying good relationships

So, what is a good, safe relationship? We've spent a lot of time discussing harm and learning to identify those who have harmful personality traits and behaviours, but focusing on the flip side of harm — the healthy — is also helpful. It allows us to reset our internal gauge and notice the principles of healthy and safe communication, therefore allowing us to better see behaviours that are unsafe. Without an experience of the positive, we are unlikely to be able to easily spot the harmful — just as we would be unlikely to truly understand the joy of happiness without a corresponding experience of sadness.

Interpersonal safety is based on the common medical principle of 'do no harm'. I like to amend this to 'do no unnecessary harm' — sometimes, harm will occur as the result of something difficult but still desirable, like providing critical feedback or ending a relationship.

Safe relationships have mutually recognised limits and boundaries, and a commitment to respectfully negotiate these boundaries. Power isn't used indiscriminately, and there are clearly agreed expectations within the relationship, as well as a shared understanding of the norms that characterise it.

The primary characteristic of relationally healthy people is their capacity to balance their own rights and needs with those of others. This is a delicate balance to find. Veering too far either way can make us either intolerably selfish and entitled or overly passive and prone to being exploited. Psychologically safe relationships allow flexibility and careful movement between the different needs of each party.

Relational safety is built upon accepting both other people and ourselves and knowing that it's impossible to be perfect. It's important to be generous of spirit, and allow people some latitude, but also to recognise if this becomes unhelpful or harmful. Relationally safe people are careful to not physically harm other people or impose on someone else's bodily space. They seek consent for any contact they have with someone else, and can clearly and openly communicate. Safe people prioritise truth and honesty, and work to communicate with honesty in ways that are not aggressive or hostile. Consistency, self-awareness, and the ability to reflect on their own behaviours, emotions, and accountabilities are all key.

A tall order?

Yes, and this is precisely why harm within relationships is so common. None of us are perfect, and we pretend that we are at our own peril. Being safe is hard — we live in a society that prioritises and values individualism, and encourages us to focus on our own needs and desires. If we're to be safe people, we must concentrate on our own behaviour first, and learn to be accountable to ourselves and others.

8

Managing Harmful People

Nina came to see me because she was being stalked. She found my private practice after hearing me speak about stalking on a podcast. *She* had identified that she was being stalked by a former colleague, Dan, but unfortunately it took more than a year for other people to put the puzzle pieces of his behaviour together, and to offer her support.

Dan was very nice to Nina when she first started working at the company. They worked in parallel roles and spent a lot of time together; this slowly evolved into what she saw as a supportive friendship. He was sometimes intense, but otherwise appeared altogether normal. The nature of their relationship changed, though, when he asked her out a few months after they started working together, and she said no. Nina was taken aback by the invitation — she wasn't romantically interested in Dan — but he took her rejection badly and stopped talking to her. He also started making inappropriate sexual remarks and jokes in her presence. She told him this made her uncomfortable, but he continued, often accompanied by pointed looks at her. This escalated once she started a relationship with someone else within the company, and she heard that he'd been telling people that she only got her promotion because she was sexually involved with a manager.

Nina reported the accusations and statements to the human resources department. Unfortunately, the HR manager was a friend of Dan's, and let him know that Nina had made a complaint but chosen not to take any formal action.

While Dan stopped speaking about Nina at work after this, she suddenly started receiving multiple obscene phone calls daily. She found out that her phone number had been placed on several public online message boards advertising sexual services. She was eventually able to get these listings removed, but continued experiencing other forms of online harassment — having redirects placed on her mail, and being signed up to email lists from sex toy companies, among others. She kept receiving phone calls, and began obsessively trawling the internet to see if her phone number or personal information had been placed on other websites. She was incredibly anxious. This continued for several months; Nina had suspicions that Dan was involved, but she had no proof.

The police laughed at Nina when she tried to report it, and her workplace told her they could take no action. They also told her that talking about it at work could be seen as her bullying or defaming Dan. Nina was distressed by the repeated intrusions into her life and worried about what Dan was capable of. She felt very nervous at work and considered changing jobs, though she didn't know if this would stop his behaviour.

Matters came to a head when Nina's social media accounts were hacked, and personal messages in her inbox were sent to all her contacts, including several intimate pictures. While this was mortifying for Nina, it also forced the police to act, as image-based abuse is illegal in Victoria. The police were able to link the hacking to Dan's IP address, and eventually charged him with stalking.

By the time Nina came to see me she was always on edge. She felt she had no control over the situation, and that no one believed her or took her seriously. She was usually quite resilient, but each time she believed Dan's behaviour had settled, something new happened. She worried that Dan's sexualised remarks would result in sexual violence directed at her. She felt like no one wanted to help her.

From a forensic psychological perspective, Dan's behaviour was problematic and fit the definition of stalking (i.e., repeated and unwanted intrusions into someone's life that may be expected to cause a reasonable person fear). It's common for people who engage in stalking behaviours to fixate on perceived offences or wrongs done to them, or to relentlessly pursue people for other ends (such as trying to have a relationship). Sometimes these fixations result in quasi-illegal behaviours, such as online or social media harassment. These behaviours are often misidentified — recognising them means seeing a *pattern* of behaviour instead of large, standalone acts. It's harder to spot patterns when you don't have all the information. It's also sadly very common to excuse or explain away some behaviours, such as sexual harassment in the workplace. Even when these patterns of behaviour *are* identified, they're often badly managed by those tasked with caring for victims, such as the HR manager at Nina's work.

People frequently struggle with knowing how to manage interactions with those who have demonstrated harmful behaviours. The reasons for this are manifold: the power differential embedded in most abusive situations; structural issues that mean someone is dependent on the perpetrator (such as a child being reliant on an abusive parent); fear of the perpetrator; fear of reprisal; uncertainty about how to respond; and difficulties with assertiveness.

The first thing to consider is whether the relationship can be managed safely by the victim alone. Where there is ongoing physical or sexual harm, I always recommend that the relationship be terminated, or supervised and managed while the perpetrator seeks treatment for their behaviours. Sometimes, I also recommend this when severe emotional harms are being perpetrated. The victim's safety is of paramount importance.

This process usually requires legal intervention and the support of other parties, such as child protection or family violence support organisations, victim support organisations, and the police. Remaining in situations with people who are harming you physically may be dangerous, and trying to manage behaviour could inflame situations because of the threat the perpetrator may feel. We know that one of the most dangerous times for women in violent relationships is when they've decided to leave — partly because the perpetrator often escalates control to try to force them to stay. Perpetrators are attuned to subtle shifts in behaviour that could signal that a victim has recognised the wrongs being done to them and may be trying to break free.

Deciding to physically leave a situation where harm is being caused is a complex process. It requires someone to acknowledge the harms and accept that they're not responsible for changing or managing a perpetrator. They will need systems of practical and emotional support, and to be able to grieve and process the loss.

This can be slow and difficult to achieve, especially if the perpetrator increases their efforts to regain control or inflicts further abuse on someone for daring to leave. Sometimes, full separation is neither possible nor desired, or we need to maintain contact for some reason — such as needing to co-parent with someone who has abused us. In these instances, there are things we can do to support safer communication, which are also helpful when managing relationships with those who *have* been harmful but have managed to reduce or cease their abusive behaviours. I discuss these in greater detail below.

Although identifying abusive behaviours is helpful, it's only the first step. Perpetrators often deny, minimise, or rationalise these behaviours. This can happen for many reasons, including the practical — avoidance of legal liability for harm caused — and less tangible reasons, such as the desire to retain prestige, or for power, esteem, or financial gain. Denial comes at a cost to the victim, though, and can make people furious, as they try to get a perpetrator to be accountable for their actions. There is no easy answer to this difficulty — there can be a range of perspectives within an interpersonally complex situation, and people have the right to defend themselves and their actions, including via legal means. Sometimes simply accepting the denial and working with it can be helpful. Ultimately, it really doesn't matter if someone denies their behaviour, as long as we can back ourselves and recognise that the same psychological tendencies that make people abuse others are likely to make them deny it as well. We do need to be believed and supported by other people in our lives, though, including those who can take action to help us.

Damaging behaviours are most often perpetrated against those with less power than the perpetrator. This power can be physical, emotional, financial, or social. It is unlikely that people will abuse those they consider equal to them, or of higher status and power. While hierarchies will continue to dominate most social structures (simply put — we need leaders and people at different levels in charge of decision-making), we can insist on harm-informed systems of power. These place clear limits on power, appoint the right types of people to positions of power, have structures of external accountability built into institutional frameworks, and zero-tolerance policies for harmful behaviours. In groups like families, this involves allowing those with less power (usually children) to have some agency and rights like the adults do, but with some boundaries to account for developmental limitations. In organisational settings, this will involve things like ensuring that bodies responsible for investigating abuses of power or corruption are external to the organisation, with no conflict of interest or vested interest in protecting the organisation or individuals within it. Those embedded within a situation simply cannot view it objectively even if they want to (and many don't want to). Institutions/groups that allow even one harmful person to continue their behaviours have effectively telegraphed, 'We don't care what happens to people; do whatever you want as long as you can hide it', to all in their ranks. It's unfortunately common for powerful people to band together to protect each other, and this can happen at all levels of society.

Addressing abuse when we see it is important. I use a 'see something, say something' model when I see someone being seriously harmed in my presence, because I have little tolerance for bad behaviours and don't want to contribute to people being harmed, whether clients, friends, colleagues, or family — silence is a form of tacit approval. I find that the best ways to address harm are directly, with the person(s) concerned, and if that doesn't work, then with those who can hold them accountable. I prefer not to use social media to call out individuals, as I have witnessed many good conversations degenerate into unproductive and nasty free-for-alls. That said, it's okay to know that we don't have the energy for certain fights sometimes, or that the costs feel bigger than the wins — and to choose to walk away to protect ourselves. At other times it may simply not be safe to intervene, such as if a solo woman notices a man behaving aggressively. Keeping oneself safe first is key, and the only reason I intervene more often than not is because a) I have specific skills in managing angry people, and b) I am incredibly tired of seeing bad behaviour occur unchecked. To put it simply, my diplomacy-dike has collapsed.

Strong boundaries
Abusive or harmful relationships have been characterised by a lack of strong boundaries, and these boundaries often need to be developed from scratch. They must involve a recognition that each person is entitled to privacy, respect, and control over their own bodies, time, energy, choices, and financial resources; we can set boundaries for ourselves, but not for others. Boundaries set the frame around a relationship and serve to keep everyone safe. Healthy relationships simply cannot exist without boundaries.

Good boundaries are aimed at protecting ourselves, not at influencing someone else's behaviour. They should be focused on the behaviours we accept and tolerate (e.g., 'I will not accept someone being physically aggressive towards me'), rather than on what other people can and cannot do ('e.g., 'People cannot speak to me rudely'). It's easy to fall into the trap of formulating boundaries that are other focused, becoming disheartened when they don't work.

Boundary formation is the first step and maintaining them requires consistent work. When people have already demonstrated tendencies to engage in harmful behaviours, entitlement and boundary breaches are likely to be part of their relational repertoire. These people will often react with anger and boundary-pushing behaviours when boundaries are introduced, and may consistently breach boundaries at first.

Holding firm to boundaries is crucial, including pointing out when one's boundaries are being breached and taking protective action. Simple statements, such as 'I don't like the way you are speaking to me. I am going to leave now and we can revisit this when things are calmer', can be helpful. Following through on statements like this is crucial; allowing boundary breaches to occur can provide a strong reinforcer for harmful behaviours. This is complex, though, and most people are inconsistent with boundaries and 'give in' when they are pushed. While good boundaries can and should be flexible, flexible boundaries should also be reserved for those with whom we already have safe and healthy relationships. The more someone pushes my boundaries, the tighter they usually become; but I have much looser boundaries with people who are close to me and have demonstrated healthy interpersonal patterns. Therapeutic support can help with responding to boundary breaches, as different responses might be needed, based on the behaviours demonstrated and the factors behind the boundary crossing.

I find it helpful to consider carefully for myself my 'firm line in the sand', and to decide what action I will take if this line is crossed. In my work with clients who have histories of aggression and violence, I often state boundaries at the outset, especially if they've previously behaved aggressively towards clinicians. I say something like:

> I am fine with you becoming angry, as anger is a natural emotion for us all to feel at times. It is fine to tell me that you are angry verbally and even to swear in our session, but I do not tolerate swearing at me, or threatening me. If this happens, we will have to stop our session for the day. I will give you one warning, but if it continues to happen, I will not be able to work with you any longer. If you ever hurt me physically, we will no longer be able to work together.

With explicitly stated boundaries like this, there are no surprises for either party, and it is easier to extricate oneself if needed, as the contract has already been agreed. The first time I had to ask a client if he was threatening me (naming a harmful behaviour is the first step to halting it), I was terrified, but it has become slightly easier with practice.

Managing interactions

We can manage abusive people by influencing the structure or the environment, including the amount of contact we have. Setting boundaries around how often we see or communicate with them can be powerful, as it allows us to conserve energy and plan interactions for times when we are most energetic, and thus able to monitor interactions and boundaries.

Even those of us who are skilled at understanding and managing human interactions and behaviours sometimes forget the importance of situational factors, such as one's environment and levels of privacy. I know of several psychologists who work from home offices, seeing clients in rooms cordoned off from their main living areas — many of these psychologists see this as an entirely expedient and tax-efficient way of conducting their work and have no qualms about the arrangement.

To someone who works in the field of forensic psychology, this feels horrifying and dangerous. I was tutored well in understanding the personal risks of my profession, and it was not long after I began studying forensic psychology that a long-term resident at Victoria's forensic psychiatric hospital stabbed his treating psychiatrist. Within my community team, I also heard about the day an eminently well-qualified psychologist was bashed by a now-notorious murderer. He was less notorious and murderous at that time, but still clearly dangerous. Those incidents, and many others like them, mean I'm acutely aware of the need to guard myself carefully. While I have long accepted that I might be stalked by a forensic client, I have no intention of making it easier for them — and safeguarding details of my personal life and home puts up a structural barrier between harm and myself. Most of the people in our lives will likely be safe (yes, even in forensic settings) but it remains difficult to predict when harm will occur — even for those of us who immerse ourselves in this world daily. Many of my more dangerous forensic clients look just like you and me — there are usually few identifiable signs that someone carries harmful impulses.

Boundaries with harmful people can involve simple steps such as having shorter phone conversations with an emotionally abusive adult, learning to end conversations when someone is heightened or aggressive, taking a support person to meetings, learning to ignore abusive text messages, ending a friendship, blocking people on social media, ensuring that conversations occur in public venues, refusing to go away on holidays with people who have demonstrated harm in the past, reducing phone communication, or ensuring that certain people don't enter our homes. These steps are not about punishing someone;

they can help enforce a manageable and safe level of contact with someone, and reduce the possibility of conflict or harm.

We can also take other practical steps, such as ensuring that we're not alone with people who have abused us and are not reliant on them for the basic goods of life (such as food or shelter). The presence of other people usually acts as a means of containment and a buffer; ensuring that we're not physically reliant on someone who has been abusive allows us to regain emotional independence. We use buffers to great effect within my forensic teams, and have found that the simple presence of an extra person in an interview room settles even the most irascible offender.

I recommend that necessary communication remain factual (such as discussing the basic facts of child access where there has been a history of intimate partner violence) and ideally is written or recorded. This allows monitoring for legal purposes if necessary and also removes the immediate emotional impact of harmful or abusive things being said verbally, and the pressure of needing to know how to respond.

Victims of abuse can become entrenched in patterns of trying to show a perpetrator how wrong their behaviour is (largely driven by their intense anguish at injustice and unfairness) but this rarely results in behaviour change or insight and can further inflame difficulties. Reinforcement (something that encourages a behaviour to continue) and punishment (something that makes it less likely that a behaviour will recur) shape behaviour: if a perpetrator is seeking something, even recognition or a strong reaction, and we provide that — their behaviour is likely to be reinforced and to continue. Removal of reinforcement — such as by providing unemotional and short responses — can act as a potent deterrent. This requires a relatively sophisticated understanding of the function (cause) of a person's behaviours, though, and it's best done in conjunction with a mental health professional who understands the drivers of specific behaviours.

Enlisting help

People frequently try to manage difficulties themselves, out of misplaced loyalty, fear, shame, worries that they won't be believed, or beliefs such as the importance of 'not airing one's dirty linen in public', but this is rarely a good idea. Enlisting help from appropriate sources is essential.

Sometimes people don't want to share details of harm they have suffered out of fear that they will be exhorted to take formal action against a perpetrator. It's a survivor's right to act as they wish — sometimes all one has the energy and capacity to do is to walk away. Other times, someone may seek redress via legal means and make formal complaints. I've done both: I've walked away, and I've chosen to make formal reports, such as with my former psychologist, largely to protect other vulnerable clients. Interestingly, several years after I finished the AHPRA notification process, I was out at dinner with friends and was talking about the problems in the therapy I had received. One of my dinner companions looked shocked and said my former psychologist's name, asking if I had seen her. I was stunned. It turned out that my friend had also seen her, received the same form of therapy, and had a similar psychological reaction — perhaps an even stronger one than mine. I was very grateful that day that I had pushed against my desire to play nice and had taken action.

Enlisting support is targeted at seeking assistance for the victim in managing behaviours, rather than at taking formal action against a perpetrator. There are a range of ways other people can support a victim: validating experiences and providing emotional support; offering practical assistance; acting as an intermediary or a buffer during interactions; and supporting a victim with protecting themselves (e.g., offering a place to stay at times of crisis). There are also formal mechanisms of redress, such as HR departments and unions for harms perpetrated within workplaces. These mechanisms aren't perfect, and victims of abuse are sometimes further targeted once they make a report, but these structures should still be considered.

Informal supports such as family and friends can reduce secrecy around abuse and help protect victims from their abusers. Abuse is always inflicted in secrecy, and by shining light on a situation, we are often able to stop or lessen the severity of the harm perpetrated. Individuals alone will never be able to change behaviours that have tacit social approval, but equally, it is important to take personal responsibility where we can and to address bad behaviour. In addition to informal supports, making sure that there are formal systems of redress is important.

Systems and organisations must create perpetrator- and harm-informed systems of support to assist people who are victimised within their care. Some of these systems are well-recognised (such as child protection), others less so. For instance, most Australian jurisdictions have poor support systems around helping people who have been stalked, and many organisations have very ineffective human resources departments and do not routinely enforce firm policies around bullying. Change must happen at a range of structural levels to create deep and lasting transformation.

Those who report abuse and harm are often identified as harmful or problematic themselves. As we say, the best defence is a good offense. This happened to me when I reported my former psychologist to the psychology board. I knew that it would likely result in suggestions that the mental health difficulties I was seeing her for had led me to misinterpret her treatment. I anguished over this, feeling sure that no one would believe me (a young, brown, mentally depleted, and relatively powerless woman) over a highly educated and powerful psychologist. This eventuated as I predicted, and her response to my complaint spoke at length about the diagnoses she thought I had and my perceived lack of readiness to engage in therapy. It was very difficult to read and felt like a huge (and low) blow — one I was prepared for but that hurt nevertheless. It is very common for cries of 'but they are mentally unwell' to be directed at people who complain. People can have mental health issues *and* correctly perceive and address injustices. Since my own experience, I have seen similar trajectories play out numerous times in other situations, especially ones where people with less power are attempting to hold those with more power and social capital to account.

A common acronym in the field of victimology is DARVO (deny, attack, and reverse victim and offender), which speaks to the way perpetrators often manage allegations. While this acronym is used perhaps a little *too* frequently and broadly, it's helpful to keep in mind when anticipating what you might encounter as you attempt to address abuse. Being aware of this helps us ensure we don't personalise it.

Responding to trauma disclosures

People are often confused about how to respond to disclosures of trauma. They can feel confronted, shocked, saddened, guilty, or angered by the things they hear. Sometimes the content matters — responses to hearing about sexual harassment at work will likely be quite different to hearing from someone that they were sexually or physically abused as a child. The emotions that come up can be similar, though, and it's these emotions that often lead to people responding in problematic ways.

These problematic responses include: dismissal ('They probably didn't mean it like that'); denial and disbelief ('He can't have raped you, why are you making it up?'), or making excuses for the perpetrator ('She must have had mental health difficulties to do that to you'). These are often motivated by defence mechanisms and a desire to believe that something so awful could never have happened; they're also common in social milieus cloaked in ideas of obedience and shame.

Supportive but excessive emotional responses can be problematic, especially if a survivor then feels responsible for caring for the person they've told. This is relatively common when relational traumas happen within a family, and when a child has been made responsible for the wellbeing of other members of the family.

When people respond to trauma disclosures in harmful ways, it can trigger some very difficult feelings for survivors. Probably the most distressing experience someone can have involves sharing a deeply painful experience and not being believed or being dismissed and invalidated. A survivor will likely have been thinking for a long time about sharing their experience and will not have made the decision lightly.

While there are many myths about trauma, statistics show that only a tiny percentage of disclosures are proven to be false, and most people who say they have experienced a trauma *have* been victimised. Overall, it is best to say something like, 'Thank you for sharing that with me, I am sorry that happened to you'.

If someone discloses a trauma to you and you experience a strong reaction, it's okay to acknowledge your own feelings to the survivor, saying something like, 'This is bringing up many feelings for me, I am sorry if I am silent as I process it'. The survivor will have their own emotions to process, so it may be more helpful to seek your own supports afterwards and keep your focus on the survivor as much as possible. Try not to ask questions — such as why you weren't told at the time of the trauma. It often takes victims many months or years to acknowledge that they were abused. This is not about the closeness of your relationship. Acknowledge that they are choosing to tell you *now*; this is powerful, and you are being given an opportunity to help someone heal.

Sometimes when people share, they want to talk about the details of what happened, and at other times they want to provide broad brushstrokes only. Either way, it's important to respect their wishes, but also to pay attention to your own emotions and needs. We all have different tolerances and capacities and I encourage everyone — survivors and supporters alike — to only ask and share explicit details of abuse with consent.

I have been in the position of receiving several unwanted trauma disclosures in social situations because of my work, and I've had to develop a range of ways to gently shut these conversations down to protect my own wellbeing when they occur without consent or foreshadowing. Something simple like, 'I'm so sorry. I know this is difficult for you to say, but I don't feel like I can absorb it right now. Is there someone else you can speak to?' — is appropriate. In my personal life, I always work with the principle of keeping myself psychologically safe *first*, so I can continue to be available to my closest people and so I can keep doing the work I do with my clients — this often means saying a respectful but firm no to others, especially around these difficult disclosures that carry great emotional weight.

Many people who have experienced trauma will have an instinctive sense of what they need from you — it may be simple acknowledgement, or it could be more complex, such as support with making a statement to the police. Some of the issues that arise can be very complicated; it's okay to give yourself time and space to absorb information before making any commitments. It may be helpful to seek your own supports, including therapeutic supports, to work through any issues that come up. These issues have no right or wrong answer, and there are different sensitivities and needs to address.

If you are in a position where you hold a duty of care to a victim, then you need to be aware of any ethical and legal responsibilities you have, such as making mandatory reports. It might be tempting to make promises you cannot keep (like agreeing that you will not tell anyone else), but your role may involve protecting the person themselves *and* protecting other people, and gentle honesty may be a better option. I have had clients ask if they can tell me things and say that I need to promise not to tell anyone else (especially in custodial settings) and I have to remind them of the duty of care I hold for them, and the environment in which I work. People are usually happy to work within these limits when they are communicated, explained, and explored. Privacy is essential for a survivor, but secrecy may not always be warranted, depending on the role you hold.

Staying within your role is important (i.e., are you receiving this disclosure as a health professional? A friend?), as is encouraging a survivor to seek appropriate supports. This does not mean brushing someone off with 'Go and speak to a psychologist' but may instead involve a careful acknowledgement that what they have shared is serious and sad, and that you want to make sure they have the best supports possible.

In responding to trauma disclousres, I'm primarily guided by the maxim of treating other people the way I would want to be treated. Through my own experiences of disclosing traumas at various times, I have learnt that the most helpful people are those who can listen without judgement, are gentle with me, and offer respect and empathy.

Managing trauma disclosures well involves clearly acknowledging what has been disclosed, offering empathy and care, being clear about the steps that need to be taken (if any) and your role, and considering follow-up care for a survivor. Hearing disclosures can be troubling, and it's important that you allow yourself to react and find your own supports as you navigate it. Give yourself permission not to get it fully right either — just trying is an excellent first step.

9

The Politics
of Trauma

You might be confused by the title of this chapter. How can trauma be political? Isn't it a psychological response to overwhelmingly distressing events? It is, but trauma is also framed by the socio-political spheres we live in.

Simple things, such as the availability of funding to treat trauma, are often political questions, contingent on election outcomes. Other, bigger issues abound — such as the types of trauma we legitimise (war) and those we prefer to ignore (child sexual abuse); the types of trauma victims we find most palatable (i.e., those most like us) and those we overlook or blame for their trauma (i.e., the majority of people in the correctional system); the perpetrators we persecute, and those we protect; the types of trauma we provide the majority of funding for treatment for (military trauma); the strictures we place around trauma victims (such as the Catholic church's non-disclosure agreements after settlements for child sex abuse); the expectations we have of those who speak about their traumas publicly (I am always struck by the huge demands we make of survivors such as Grace Tame and Rosie Batty); the manner in which we allow and even encourage certain systems to retraumatise people; and those victims we often simply refuse to see (such as boys and men), perhaps out of embedded beliefs about the invulnerability of certain groups, or concern that legitimising harms done to men will detract from our growing awareness of harms done to women.

Our responses to all this will be informed by our upbringing, our political leaning, the family within which we were raised, the legal systems, prevailing social norms, and our own innate emotional patterns. Trauma is a hot-button topic, and the issues raised here are complex.

I am often alarmed by the ways we fail trauma victims. We fail to recognise and validate their experiences and we fail to adequately support them — despite frequent conversations about the importance of trauma-informed care. For true systems of trauma-informed care and a better trauma-informed society, we need to look at the gaps in our knowledge and at the biases we bring, as confronting as this is.

The first time I felt I was failing a traumatised client was in my work as a family violence case manager. I worked for a feminist family violence agency in Melbourne — almost all the family violence services operating in Australia work within a strict feminist approach, and use an ideology that positions intimate partner violence (IPV; I prefer this phrase, as family violence is broad and encompasses numerous relationships) as a choice men make, and a choice that's based on patriarchal social norms of men's power and control over women. The Duluth[1] model — founded on a very small study conducted in 1980s Minnesota — was the only model I was trained in, and provided the explanation (i.e., IPV is based on men's power and control over women) I shared with my clients. It was based exclusively on intimate partner violence, and came from research conducted in a monocultural, socially conservative context in America with a small handful of heterosexual women and men. From this meagre and unrepresentative beginning, we have built the bulk of our current work in the field of family violence in Australia, including services designed to support victims, and interventions designed to help perpetrators change their behaviours.

The term 'men's power and control' and the related term 'gendered violence' are often used but are quite vague.

What does 'power and control' mean? How do we measure power? Is every couple beset by this power differential? If power does indeed cause violence, does it mean that every parent will abuse their child (since adults tend to have power over children)? Have power balances shifted since the Duluth research was completed over 40 years ago? How do we explain violence in child–parent relationships, sibling relationships, or same sex relationships? What about elder abuse? Are there different factors that cause IPV in Aboriginal communities? What about culturally and linguistically diverse (CALD) communities such as South Asian groups where issues like dowry are a factor? What makes power tip into violence? If IPV is about men's power, how do we explain female-perpetrated violence? Do we believe that female-perpetrated violence exists? If IPV is about social norms, is every man fated to play these norms out in their intimate relationships? If not, what sets apart men who *are* violent towards women, from those who are *not*? Is there any difference between an unwell man who might kill his mother during a psychotic episode, a stepfather who sexually abuses his stepdaughter, and the man who hits his partner because he is angry and can't manage emotion? Are all these different types of gendered crimes caused by power differentials? Are risk levels the same? What risks are we worried about? What treatment will each of these men need?

These are uncomfortable questions, but are nevertheless important ones, and ones we consider daily in forensic work.

In my case management role, I was known as a 'domestic violence advocate'. People in this role supported women with organising the minutiae of their life and finding safety as they tried to leave violent relationships. And as a state-funded family violence organisation, despite only being trained in the Duluth model, we were tasked with remedying *all* forms of family violence — child-to-parent violence, violence between same-sex partners, violence between siblings and extended family members, and any aggressive behaviours perpetrated by ex-partners (forensically, this is 'stalking', and comes with somewhat different risk factors).[2] Parent-to-child violence fell within the ambit of child protection services, who worked with different ideological frameworks, more aligned with the multifactorial models we use in the field of forensic psychology.

So, while we ostensibly worked with victims of all types of family violence, we could only offer the 'power and control' explanation for these behaviours. We worked solely with female victims — I remain unsure what support services male victims[3] access, as all services in Victoria at the time of writing are geared towards the needs of female victims. There were two acute failures in this role that led to me leaving this work and studying forensic psychology, to find broader ways of understanding and changing harmful behaviours.

The first occurred when I was speaking to a 65-year-old woman who was experiencing severe difficulties with her 33-year-old son. He had a diagnosis of schizophrenia, and was aggressive to her and very sexually threatening when he was becoming unwell — she often had to lock herself into her bedroom at night. She was loath to live with him but equally loath to have him removed from her home, knowing it would send him into a spiral of homelessness and substance use. Intervention orders were of no use to her, and she refused police intervention for similar reasons. She cried on the phone to me, asking if we could work with him to help him. She had done the rounds of mental health services, but he refused to work with them and was not unwell enough (yet) to warrant compulsory treatment.

Unfortunately not, I had to say — we couldn't work with perpetrators, and men were not allowed in the building, unless conducting essential work. Most family violence services have exemptions from discrimination legislation so they can hire female staff only to work with victims, and most services don't work with men at all, with some refuges even stopping older adolescent boys from accompanying their mothers into shelters. All this raises some interesting dilemmas around managing the needs of gender-diverse and non-binary people (Victoria has since developed a few new state-funded services for LGBTIQA+ survivors of IPV). It also disempowers female victims, with the underlying view that they're helpless and need to be protected from all men. There is the tacit understanding that men are the 'other' — even victimised teenage boys accompanying their mothers. This is quite a different paradigm to the one I utilise now when working with trauma survivors as a psychologist. We are clear that avoidance of trauma triggers, including avoiding broad groups such as men, will often contribute to the development and maintenance of PTSD[4]. I thus work with clients to create realistic beliefs (e.g., 'some men have been harmful to me, but others have been safe' vs. 'all men are dangerous'), and to reduce avoidance.

I offered to refer this client's son to a Men's Behaviour Change program — an intervention program holding perpetrators of violence accountable for their actions through a power and control lens. I didn't think this was a suitable intervention — the man was clearly very unwell, and was himself traumatised (he'd been subject to recurring violence from his deceased father and had been sexually abused as a child), and was a heavy substance user — but it was all I had. She kept crying, as she asked me to explain why he did what he did to her, when all she was trying to do was provide a safe home for him. 'Men's power and control over women ...' I said, tailing off weakly. She ended the call soon afterwards, still crying, and then refused to accept further phone calls. My answer did not even scratch the surface, but I had no alternative to offer at that time.

The second instance of failure came when I began working with a woman who wanted to leave her husband after years of insidious control. His behaviours towards her and their children were truly awful, and masked well behind the veil of a 'nice' man — no one else knew what was occurring, as is common with IPV and coercive control. When she left him, she worried that he would kill himself — he had said he wanted to die. I identified this as another attempt to control her — as we were taught to do when working with perpetrators who talk of suicide. I advised her to contact emergency services if she was concerned. This was cold comfort for her when he killed himself. At that time, I saw his act as an expression of anger and ultimate control; but now I look back with some horror and a deep sense of regret. Acts of suicide (which are different to threats of suicide) are never a form of control; control entails needing to be alive and this man had chosen a form of suicide that was sure to end his life. He was anguished yes, perhaps angry, likely devastated by the loss of his role in the family, exposure of his actions, and his sudden awakening to the cost of his actions — but this was an act of despair, not control.

Shortly after, I left my role. I still think about that family, wishing I'd had some of the knowledge I have now so I could have better helped them. I may not have been able to prevent the outcome, but a more decisive intervention at that time might have helped him get the support he clearly needed and lightened the burden his wife and children now carry.

I experienced many such moments, trying to use this limited paradigm to explain violence in same-sex or gender-diverse relationships, harm perpetrated by siblings towards each other, harms perpetrated by adolescent/adult children (male and female) towards their parents, and financial control perpetrated by adult children towards elder parents, as well as other episodes of clear bidirectional violence in heterosexual relationships. Some of our clients were indeed victims of patriarchal terrorism[5] (the coercive control we often hear described in cases like the murder of Hannah Clarke and her children), but it was not the case for all.

I want to be clear that women *are* at greater risk of physical violence (especially lethal violence and intimate partner homicide) in intimate relationships than men, and that much of this violence is gendered (i.e., perpetrated by men against women). However, just because this violence is gendered doesn't mean that gender norms alone *cause* it. Some of the answers lie in other arenas, such as the way men are socialised to manage emotion, or early experiences of intergenerational trauma (for instance, witnessing parental IPV, or parental histories of war trauma). Nor does gendered violence mean that men don't experience IPV or other forms of abuse as victims. There is clearly something very problematic in gender relationships in our society, and family violence organisations do excellent work to protect many women — we need these organisations and their views — but we also need to look much more broadly to truly catalyse change.

Many women are harmed by men, some men are harmed by women, some men are harmed by men, not all men harm, and some men harm. These are not mutually exclusive facts, and acknowledging each of them as reality doesn't negate the hurt done to individual victims. Unfortunately, the current public discourse is characterised by polarisations, enormous anger, and the firm need to pick a side. Any discussion about violence against women is met with cries of 'Not all men', and equal amounts of vitriol are directed towards men whenever a serious crime against a woman hits the headlines. I'm often reminded of the rhetoric of 'If you're not with us, you're against us' when witnessing this, and these polarities don't appear to do much except ensure that we remain locked in stasis with our interventions.

Division and rage are common when there has been great hurt, as is the experience of many survivors of IPV.

IPV is no different to any other form of violence or harm, insofar as it requires careful psychological analysis and multi-pronged treatment and intervention approaches.[6] Numerous factors contribute to intimate partner violence, one of which is gender norms. Women are at higher risk of physical violence and lethal violence — but swathes of emerging research point to the bidirectional nature of many forms of IPV,[7] including emotional and verbal abuse, and the need to broaden our understanding of IPV to look at the complex individual dynamics occurring in each couple,[8] as well as all the different forces that can lead to violence. Factors such as early childhood experiences, attitudes around the use of violence to resolve difficulties, substance use, mental health difficulties, cognitive difficulties, poor emotional control, impulsivity, life stressors, poor insight, and personality disorders all influence the development of violent behaviour. All these elements must be considered in tandem when understanding IPV, assessing risk, and determining interventions. Gender norms might be applicable in many cases, but they are *not* the sole cause of IPV.

Examining and treating misogynistic attitudes is a common part of any forensic assessment I undertake when violence is perpetrated against women, including partner violence and sexual violence. Most sexual violence is perpetrated by men against women, and understanding attitudes allowing this are a key part of interventions, but understanding attitudes is a *part* of my assessment and treatment, not the whole.

As a woman, and as a feminist working in the field of forensic psychology, I inhabit a difficult space. I spent twelve years of my early life in New Delhi, a city often colloquially called the 'rape capital of the world'. I am no stranger to the anguish and harm men can cause. However, I also grew up hearing about dowry deaths, and witnessed a close family friend experience systematic abuse by her mother-in-law, until the mother-in-law tried to kill our family friend by setting her on fire. The mother-in-law missed, set herself on fire accidentally, sustained third-degree burns, and died. Men *can* be abusive and harmful, but there are other stories, too, and the overall picture is often far more complex.

I often find that our conversations about IPV and gendered violence in Australia have a race problem. The specific circumstances and needs of Aboriginal women and women from culturally diverse backgrounds are only just starting to be acknowledged. Deaths of women of colour are often ignored by the media. Many Aboriginal women are misidentified as perpetrators when IPV happens in their relationships (often perpetrated by their white male partners), perhaps because they can sometimes have harsh histories and may resemble the 'difficult trauma victim' I described in Chapter 5. Women from CALD backgrounds (like Indian women) are often controlled by other women in their own homes, such as mothers-in-law and sisters-in-law. Matters like dowry and family 'izzat' (honour and shame) are important ones to discuss, as are the cultural and family pressure to make a relationship work at all costs.

White feminists and activists often push for a policing response (e.g., laws against coercive control) and tend to fail to acknowledge any of these diverse experiences. While I believe that IPV is a crime and requires a strong policing response, I also hold in mind the great harms visited on Aboriginal communities by the police, and the reluctance many Aboriginal people have to involve the police. In addition, asking untrained police to determine such complex circumstances as whether emotional abuse is occurring in a relationship strikes me as a recipe for disaster.

We already have the laws, tools, and access to the knowledge we need to change our responses to IPV and bring them in line with forensic best practice; we are just choosing not to yet — whether out of lack of commitment, dogged adherence to an ideology, lack of funding, a belief that in some ways IPV is a women's problem to be solved by women's services, or other factors entirely.

When interventions are based only on changing the gender norms underlying family violence, they are helpful *if* these norms are the primary factor. However, using these interventions when there are other factors underlying IPV is like treating a broken leg with cholesterol medication — entirely ineffective. For most high-risk offenders, gender norms will not be the central cause of escalating violence, or the immediate intervention target to stop a homicide — they will typically be a background predisposing factor.

When we resort to ideological models of explanation, and adhere to these firmly, without being able to look at research and changing social norms, we fail victims. Our multicultural, intersectional, and gender-diverse society is very different to the society of Duluth, Minnesota, in the 1980s, with different difficulties underpinning abuse — and we would do well to evolve our understanding of behaviour as societies progress and norms change. Our societies have altered hugely since the 80s, and it feels like an oversight to assume that the same factors underpin behaviours, despite the intervening decades.

We fail victims when we cannot understand and explain behaviours adequately, and we fail victims when we have limited mechanisms of protection. We fail victims when we cannot offer good, tested treatments to perpetrators that work to reduce behaviours, and I suspect the lack of appropriate treatment for recidivist offenders — beyond the largely untested gender norm–focused Men's Behaviour Change programs — is at least partially why we see continuously rising rates of IPV. It is becoming increasingly well recognised that interventions for IPV must be informed and supported by those who are trained in working with perpetrators. While the legal and court systems have slowly started to adopt this view, it has not yet resulted in any changes in treatments offered for IPV. We have a range of forensically informed programs (one size never fits all) offered for other types of crime (such as sexual and violent crimes), but IPV lags — which in some ways reflects the lack of seriousness with which we have historically approached this form of offence, and the assumption that this is a problem for the victims and victim support agencies to manage themselves.

I've noticed that the rhetoric around an IPV-related homicide is often 'why wasn't he locked up?' People often forget that we can't simply be locked up unless we have already done something serious to warrant removal of liberty. Locking people up has serious consequences for them. I worked in the prison system after the tightening of Victoria's bail laws in 2018 and found that reams of women (most often Aboriginal women) were entering prison on remand (i.e., not having yet been found guilty or sentenced) for petty offences such as stealing food, because they were caught in these tightened laws. By entering prison, women often lose their housing, access to mental health services, and their children. Sometimes when we move to incarceration as a knee-jerk response, we forget that people who are innocent are also caught in this punishing response — including the very people we may want to protect.

This isn't to say we can't intervene in high-risk cases: bringing forensic psychological and criminological expertise to bear on risk assessment and management; closely monitoring those offenders identified as being high risk; and working with victim support agencies — these are all ways we can better manage risk and reduce the likelihood of IPV homicide. This risk, however, will never be eliminated completely, for several reasons — it's hard to predict something with a low base rate (as an example, how good would we be at predicting whether lightning will strike somewhere twice?), and we don't know which factors reliably differentiate between the risk of non-homicidal IPV and homicidal IPV.

We *do* know that there are a few pathways[9] to intimate partner homicide (most often perpetrated by men against female partners), which helps us make some assessments of risk. For instance, looking at the types of intimate partner homicide perpetrators tells us that Hannah Clarke's murderer[10] fit into the fixated-threat pathway[11] and that intelligence-led policing in conjunction with frontline support may have been beneficial. This means we have to focus on accurately determining who is at high risk, understanding pathways, and working with high-risk victims and offenders as though there is the potential for homicide. This needs a good risk assessment tool. Creating and validating (i.e., testing) risk assessment tools is a very complex statistical process, and does not simply mean saying 'well, what do *we* think the risk markers are?'

This 'design-by-committee' approach is how tools in the IPV field such as the Common Risk Assessment Framework (CRAF) in Victoria were created, and this may be why so many high-risk cases are misidentified. Risk assessment in the field of IPV currently sits approximately 20 years behind the risk assessments we have for other offending behaviours. If a tool is poorly formulated, we don't know what it actually tests (risk of *something* happening? Risk of violence? Risk of homicide?) and victims who are at high risk may be identified as being at low risk (possibly resulting in death), and vice versa. We must be able to differentiate between risk levels, because the most high-risk offenders and victims need the most intervention and support, and we need to know how to allocate resources. We simply don't have the resources to offer the same interventions to everyone, nor is this helpful.[12]

We also fail victims when we discount the terrors they face or brush their concerns away — as we have done with both family violence and child sexual abuse. We fail victims when we refuse to see them or to provide support to *all* victims, and this occurs sometimes with male victims of certain forms of harm, including intimate partner violence and child sexual abuse.[13] It was not long ago that we did the same to victims of paedophile priests within the Catholic church, regardless of their gender.

I have worked with many male victims, and a common narrative thread is that they often did not report their abuse[14] or seek support because of shame, lack of recognition of abuse, concern that they would not be believed, the actuality that they were *not* believed, and lack of appropriate services and pathways. This difficulty acknowledging that men are abused as well, and acknowledging their psychological needs, is at odds with our focus on preventing violence, given the established links between experiencing and witnessing abuse or violence in childhood and later perpetration of violence.[15]

The facts are stark and simple — many boys (and girls)[16] witness and experience violence as children, including violence within their families — and some of these boys (and girls) will go on to perpetrate violence in their own lives and within their own families, often at least partially influenced by the trauma they experienced. We cannot see these children as victims, and then suddenly move to seeing them as perpetrators once they turn 18 — which is what currently happens within legal and social services systems. Youth services are oriented towards seeing younger people who harm as requiring support, not punishment; and concerted efforts are made to understand, support, and rehabilitate. However, most of these services abruptly flip once someone is legally an adult, though they still have an adolescent brain[17] — and the emphasis is then on locking them up. The boys we worked with as child victims within the family violence and child protection systems are labelled perpetrators once they turn 18, if displaying the aggression they learnt to use in their families. Many of these children start to attract police attention and formal charges in adolescence, as they enact the traumas they experienced.[18]

We fail victims with our binaries of age, our divisions into victim and perpetrator. We fail them when we forget to look at the broader sphere of someone's life and at the different roles they take on in different relationships. We fail them by labelling and pigeonholing, trapping people in a certain system.

The rate of trauma among male prisoners is very high — approximately 56 per cent of the male prison population[19] has been found to meet the threshold for a diagnosis of PTSD (with even more demonstrating subthreshold symptoms), and many of these men cycle through the prison system with no understanding of the impact of their trauma histories on their mental health, their emotional and self-regulation skills, and their interpersonal capacities. All these factors are relevant to why someone might offend, and by ignoring the basic fact of these trauma histories, we often allow cycles of reoffending to continue.

We fail trauma victims when we do not identify them, and when we do not provide appropriate care — whether that's therapeutic care or support to achieve basic life goals. And we fail them when they are retraumatised by the systems designed to protect them. This can occur in a range of ways and is a feature of many systems — policing, correctional, child protection, and disability care. It often occurs through harsh, punitive environments directed at containment or punishment. Clear examples are apparent in practices such as the overuse of seclusion rooms and restraints in mental health services, strip searches in prison, and overuse of chemical restraints in disability support services. Other examples are more subtle: such as insisting that patients in psychiatric hospitals are 'manipulating' or 'splitting staff', when their behaviours are just adaptive strategies they have built to seek support and manage traumas and difficult lives. Similarly, it's common to hear the word 'manipulation' used in the prison system. It's entrenched in the attitudes and enshrined in all the training literature, and can result in behaviours that retraumatise, such as unnecessary strip searches[20] or overzealous use of isolation cells.[21] When people are retraumatised by systems designed to help and support, it compounds their initial trauma and increases distress and suspicion, separating them from those who are meant to help. We need trauma-informed systems of care to ensure that we don't inadvertently retraumatise those we are trying to help.

Finally, we fail victims when we see traumas and injustices and allow them to continue. This is why I've broken out of the neutrality often expected of a psychologist and taken a firmer and stronger stance against all forms of harm, regardless of the nature or gender of the perpetrator. The neutrality of earlier times has not worked to effect change. Psychology was born in a polite sociocultural cauldron, but times (and therapists) have vastly evolved since then; and the world needs more than just neutrality or politeness. We have made great strides, yes, but there's a lot more to be done, and those of us who have voices and the desire to use them must be able to do so in the service of making the world a safer and relationally healthier place. Noticing when harms occur and being able to understand them and meaningfully address them is important.

Call-out social media culture has very limited utility — the more people pile onto a person, the more entrenched their views will likely become (and we don't want to become abusive ourselves in the pursuit of 'justice') — but directly addressing harms we see as soon as we can is important. It's easy to let things slide — safer and more comfortable — and easy to believe that the small injustices and hurts inflicted do not matter.

They do; and what we do matters.

10

Caring for the Carer

In 2021, I ran a workshop on being a forensic psychologist for clinicians interested in the field. One of the attendees asked me about vicarious occupational trauma, and I spoke about it briefly and ended with a blithe comment about not having experienced vicarious trauma yet, and said I would revisit the question in a few years (forgetting about the times work had already evoked trauma responses in me) — once I had some firsthand knowledge of it.

I should know by now that saying something like this is asking for trouble. I've been told off many times for walking onto our unit at work and noting that it was 'quiet' — we all hold the firm, magical belief that as soon as we say something like this, chaos will descend. In this instance, it was only a few months later that I found myself sitting awake, anxiously watching my front door. I had spent a few days immersed in thinking about a forensic client who had very vivid fantasies of homicide and desires to murder people; and late one night I experienced a sudden terrifying image (an intrusion, in post-traumatic terminology) of him bursting through my front door with a weapon.

I knew what had brought it on: I was tired, so tired, after two years of pandemic living and working; I was burnt out from working for six days a week across three different roles; I hadn't been tending to myself in the usual ways (yoga, time away, non–psychology related light reading, scheduled time in nature). My clients seemed higher risk than usual, and though we are used to carrying a level of risk in forensic work, this was beginning to grate. It is a big responsibility, to know that someone may kill or rape someone if you miss something or fail to pick up on a sign. I was feeling isolated and lonely after repeated lockdowns and against this background, had driven past the area where my client had recently tried to assault someone. While nothing (thankfully) had eventuated from this attempt, I still felt a chill as I thought of the murderous impulses he carried and how bad it could have been. I let my mind wander to imagining the scene — and this is something I never do, knowing how visual my brain is, and how quickly these tendrils can wrap around my thoughts. I violated my own rule, and briefly paid the price. Luckily, because I am aware of vicarious trauma and aware that I'll experience it, I had some sense of how to manage it, and was able to shake it off relatively quickly by heading off on a large, planned chunk of leave shortly after. Nonetheless, it was a reminder for me.

Being a woman in the world of forensic psychology has some unique challenges, including hearing, almost constantly, about the many twisted ways men can violate women, and having to carefully watch dynamics in the therapy room to ensure that my client is not drawing me into the abusive patterns he's inflicted on others. Some of my female colleagues who work with male sex offenders experience having their boundaries crossed, and egregious intrusions — such as a client masturbating in their presence. Something similar happened to me, when a man I was assessing for telephone scatalogia (obscene phone calls) started making personal comments about my appearance, comparing me to the first woman he had sex with. He was clearly sexually aroused. There is a specific violation you feel when you experience something like this in a professional capacity, and when it happened to me, I was shaken for days. As a result of instances like this, I am acutely attuned to the need to balance my thinking, so that I don't stomp around in a fit of misandrist rage (and yes, this does involve reminding myself 'Not all men'), and am still able to acknowledge the many kind and ethical men I know. This emotional and mental work is constant, is often very poorly acknowledged by forensic and correctional services, and is an extra burden to carry, especially when I bump up against several male clients all at once who want to abuse women.

There's little research into the ways in which female practitioners process this onslaught, or the differences between the moral injuries done to male and female clinicians who hear about these cases. 'Moral injury' refers to the strong cognitive and emotional responses that occur when someone is forced to participate in or witness behaviour that violates their moral code. In the forensic world, there are times when clients elicit this reaction — I've had a client say 'she asked for it', when their victim was aged just six, and this brought up many emotions that required processing in my own time. The effort to respond in a neutral and non-judgemental way while not colluding or accepting these statements can use massive amounts of energy. At other times, it is the setting itself that causes the moral injury — such as when mental health clinicians work in settings like prisons, which tend to be geared towards punishment, not recovery, or see injuries done to colleagues in work teams characterised by bullying, harassment, and violence.

Vicarious trauma means the cumulative trauma we experience when we work with those who have experienced traumatic events, or are repeatedly exposed to information about traumatic events, as with police officers who view child exploitation material as part of their efforts to infiltrate paedophile rings and stop the production and download of this material. Vicarious trauma comes from bearing witness to suffering and pain, and needing to emotionally process traumatic material, even if these traumas were not directly inflicted on oneself. It is important to differentiate between vicarious/

occupational trauma, burnout (i.e., being overwhelmed by chronic workplace stress and workload), and compassion fatigue (i.e., emotional and physical exhaustion leading to a reduced capacity to feel empathy and compassion). While any profession can experience vicarious trauma or burnout, professions involving direct client work (such as psychology, law, and medicine) also bring attendant risks of compassion fatigue. It's impossible to enter the world of people who hurt each day, and to give full and sustained attention to them, without feeling some of what they feel.

Many people are vulnerable to vicarious trauma, including anyone who hears about traumatic events as part of their work: doctors, allied health professionals, psychiatrists, psychologists, counsellors, and clergy. Family and friends are not exempt either, which is why I encourage victims to seek consent before sharing explicit details of their traumas with their personal supports.

Some professionals directly witness extremely disturbing things in their line of work — consider emergency responders such as paramedics, fire brigades, and forensic cleaners. Others experience serious occupational violence themselves — correctional officers, police, residential care workers, and child protection workers. Most first responders will experience a level of vicarious trauma through witnessing the suffering of victims, but can also suffer direct trauma, through occupational violence, being involved in aggression, or witnessing violent acts. All these forms of occupational trauma can be conceptualised as a subtype of relational trauma, occurring as they do within the structure of workplace relationships.

It's important to remember that people (even psychologists) can develop PTSD from vicarious or direct workplace exposure to trauma. People should always be screened for PTSD when they start displaying trauma or mood symptoms in any line of work that involves exposure to harm or violence. Occupational trauma can be deeply problematic — it's not a simple thing that can be managed with cupcakes, yoga, or classes in resilience. Resilience is a corporate buzzword at present. It's a misnomer and a convenient way for corporations and organisations to shift responsibility for wellbeing onto the individual. While individuals can work to strengthen themselves, they also need good, supportive systems, fair pay, and manageable workloads. When I stumble across organisations that ask workers what they can do to support themselves when exposed to troubling material, I usually throw the question back at them and ask what they do to support their staff who are exposed to troubling material. I'm quite a hit with employers. There is a high rate of PTSD diagnoses within certain subsets of first responders,[1] including the police and paramedics; I have treated some myself. Engaging in these lines of work involves the tacit acceptance that one will see and be exposed to certain things, and it can come as a surprise when the cumulative effects of harm prove too much to bear. First responders often lack training in understanding and acknowledging mental health, and work within a culture where stoicism is encouraged and emotional expression is disallowed. These cultures are also hierarchical, and often have bullying and harassment embedded within them. Add in shift work and disturbed circadian cycles, postings and deployments that remove people from their usual supports, secrecy around work (such as when working with operationally sensitive material) and needing to carry the emotional impacts of the work alone, and it's no surprise that many people within these professions fail to manage vicarious trauma well.

The challenges are different for other professions. Psychologists for instance tend to sacrifice themselves easily. Most of us deeply want to help people and thus extend ourselves, forgetting that this work demands so much from us anyway that we often have no extra to give. Perhaps we think that we won't get PTSD, because we know all the symptoms. If extended too far, all it takes is something simple — an angry or abusive client, that final request for extra work, a vexatious complaint to the licensing board — for people to crack. Difficulties like compassion fatigue can strike at the very heart of the work a psychologist does, and can evoke great shame. These issues are not often spoken about because of this shame. Opening the door to these conversations can help people realise they are not alone and that these responses are almost inevitable when one is immersed in such difficult and emotionally demanding work.

On the other hand, people can cope with surprisingly large amounts of trauma if they are well supported, feel like they are doing meaningful work, have a sustainable workload, and perceive that they are valued at work. Recognition of the risks involved in this work is increasing, and great inroads have been made into mitigating them within the Victorian police force and paramedicine.

Other sectors are lagging — the ADF, for example — and there's almost no recognition of the trauma and aggression experienced by those who work in the legal and correctional systems and with families and children in care, including child protection workers, youth justice workers, correctional officers, and residential care workers. It's common that they're exposed to serious occupational violence from clients and traumatised (and angry) families — and I have seen many of them resign (at best) or have to take months of sick and stress leave.

Recently, a solicitor, Zagi Kozarov, successfully sued her employer for PTSD she sustained while working in the sex crimes division of the Office of Public Prosecutions in Victoria. They initially denied her claim, requiring that she take the matter all the way to the High Court. This is a really important case and one I have followed with interest. I have observed that organisations largely prefer not to take responsibility for the harms people experience at work, or the contribution of issues such as poor management practices or overwork to the development of PTSD. It's been easy to blame those who sustain psychological injuries at work ('maybe they were predisposed to trauma') and ignore these issues when people quietly faded into the background. Now that people are fighting back and there is media attention, legal support, and financial penalties for negligence or lack of support, it is likely that employers will be gradually forced to up their game.

There are multiple factors that contribute to high rates of traumatisation at work: the belief that one should subjugate their own needs to protect clients; the belief that certain clients (e.g., young people) are incapable of hurting adults (the one time I was physically injured at work, it was when four rather stocky knife-wielding ten-year-olds pushed me down a flight of stairs); unrealistic expectations that place the entire responsibility for saving people onto workers; a punitive and retributive system focused on apportioning blame and protecting itself ('You don't want to end up in front of the Coroners Court' is a dictum I often heard in child protection); and encouragement of unsustainable work hours are just some of them. Sometimes, people were physically injured in catastrophic ways and even those who did not sustain physical injuries were commonly pushed to the very limits of their capabilities by systems structured around blame, overwork, and callous disregard for the people involved.

Long-term exposure to trauma without adequate supports typically results in a range of difficulties, including cynicism, fatigue, desensitisation to harms, and dehumanisation of clients. This occurs across many law enforcement and correctional settings, where staff have to learn to see and treat their clients as somehow *less than* in order to work within a system designed to punish. Once we stop seeing distress and responding to it as a human would — with some care and empathy — we have entered dangerous territory. To a certain extent, desensitisation is adaptive — I could not do my job if I flinched every time I heard the word 'rape' — but when it goes too far, it can become callous. It's a fine balance to strike and one that requires much training, understanding of why people behave as they do, and capacity and time to reflect — none of which are provided to those who are on the frontline of most responses.

My first experience of vicarious trauma occurred when I was a brand-new helpline volunteer at a mental health crisis support line. I was warned that there was a menace caller — people often called to harass the telephone counsellors, especially men who telephoned later at night to engage in very unpleasant sexually harassing behaviours towards the mostly female workforce. On this occasion, the person telephoned from a geographically remote region (making it easy to identify when he called), ostensibly to talk about grief around family law and custody issues, but quickly escalating into talking about guns, knives, and slashing people, including the volunteer on the phone to him. This wouldn't really upset me now, but it was certainly not part of my training as a first-year undergraduate psychology student. I had a phone call with him, ended the call quickly as per our management protocol, and then went home and had a nap — waking in tears after a nightmare about someone chasing me with a knife. It was not hard to make the connection. Luckily, the helpline had drilled into us the inevitability of having an unexpectedly difficult reaction to a call and had set out clear ways to manage this, including telephoning the on-call supervisor for a debrief. I did so, talked about the call in enough depth to allow my mind to process it, spoke about my emotions and worries, and was reassured about the actions I had taken. That human contact and being able to normalise my feelings, process the experience, and co-regulate helped me manage it quickly, and I had no further reactions to the call.

Often, people in helping professions have beliefs that encourage the development of vicarious trauma. These beliefs can hinge around invulnerability ('This should not upset me', 'I don't get upset', 'I need to manage this alone'), self-sacrifice ('I need to keep going even if I am upset; other people have it worse than I do', 'I can't stop, other people need me'), weakness ('If I show I am upset, it means I am weak and can't do this job'), stoicism ('I can't cry at work'), and perfectionism ('I need to solve everything for everyone, all the time', 'If I just do the right things, the outcome will be fine'). I know I have these tendencies myself, and they are surprisingly hard to push against. It's easy to say no in theory but much harder when you are trying to say no to a specific client in need. I'm slowly learning to build a buffer of space around myself, knowing my bent towards self-sacrifice and invulnerability. This may look like booking in one less client a day, saying no to seeing an aggressive client, or working for a smaller fraction.

In reality, working with human beings is messy and difficult, and good outcomes are not guaranteed, despite our best efforts. Working in the social services and health spheres means we acknowledge the risks and the certainty of some adverse outcomes, while doing what we can to counter these risks. This is hard to maintain, though, and it's common for people to either become blasé and accept injuries and deaths, or (more commonly), to believe that they are at fault if they cannot prevent an adverse outcome.

Noticing and responding to difficult reactions early is key, and seeking support from those qualified to help allows us to cognitively make sense of a traumatic event before it takes root. This can act as a buffer, preventing the development of PTSD. When I work with first responders with PTSD, I remind them that they will inevitably experience another traumatic event as part of their work, so it's important to remember and keep practising the cognitive and emotional management skills we've worked on in therapy, to protect against retraumatisation.

Addressing the belief patterns people hold is important, but setting up structures that allow people the space and time they need to process things can be difficult when the demands of their organisations and workplaces mean that rest is frowned upon. Many healthcare workers (including myself) are very fatigued after more than three years of managing a pandemic, and many have not taken a break, instead continuing to tend to the needs of other people. This has been reinforced by a public who have deified us as 'heroes', forgetting that we are *just* people. Many workplaces have focused on 'business as usual', forgetting there has been nothing usual about this time. For some, this has led to complete burnout, resulting in people leaving the profession in droves. While this is occurring at such a scale now that we cannot help but notice it, there has always been slow attrition from the health and caring professions, driven by burnout and occupational traumas.

The second time I experienced an episode of work-related trauma was when I worked in child protection and lead tenant care during my doctorate in psychology. Lead tenancies are systems set up to support older adolescents in care into independent living in Australia, usually between the ages of 16 to 18 (with the intention that they are unceremoniously evicted from state care on their eighteenth birthday). In theory, this allows younger people to develop the skills they need to live independently, under the guidance of two volunteers who live at the property rent-free, while going about their normal lives. Unfortunately, this system was used inappropriately by child protection, and some of their most troubled and high-risk youth were placed there (seemingly when staffed residential care houses tired of managing them). Low-risk placements like this are intended for low-risk youth, typically those without histories of significant violence, mental health issues, or substance use. Most adolescents would struggle to live alone at age 16, let alone those with severe trauma histories.

During my lead tenant role, I had a young person with significant methamphetamine use and a history of serious assaults placed with me. The placement quickly descended into chaos, with an utter lack of safety for all residing there. Methamphetamine was used (and likely sold) at the house, adult male strangers descended on the property at all hours, police attended almost daily, angry neighbours threatened to punch me because of the neighbourhood disturbances, and the young person herself assaulted me — and seriously assaulted other people in my presence. I was terrified.

It was chaos, and the system was lucky that no one was hurt or died. She was a young person ill-equipped to make good life choices and was reactive and troubled, managing things in the only way she knew. The people who failed were those in the child protection system who made poor decisions about where she would be placed, and then ignored the escalating chaos because it was easier to do so ('Don't escalate her' was a refrain I heard, which seemed to translate to 'Don't set any limits, because she gets very angry when we do'). While it may seem a kindness to allow someone a chance at living independently, the 16-year-old traumatised and drug-affected brain is unable to cope with this, and has none of the capacities required to regulate. External containment and strict structures are needed; and lead tenant living, with its emphasis on independence, had none.

Having few limits and boundaries for clients is common in child protection (the much-vaunted phrase in Victoria, the 'child's best interests' seems to have acquired this meaning, though children and adolescents need firm limits for optimum functioning) and means that young people are allowed to make terrible decisions, and are drawn further into a vortex of trauma as they are preyed upon by malignant individuals.

When working in a paid capacity in child protection, I would routinely have 13-year-olds leave the house in the wee hours of the night, and often saw them collected by older men in cars. I had no power to stop them from leaving the house or to monitor them or their social media/phones in any capacity; I was only able to report them as missing to the police, who would sigh wearily — having already received three reports about this adolescent over the week prior. They usually returned, sometimes flush with drugs and money, at other times with stories of having been hurt or raped. This happened weekly, and on this tenuous tightrope of repeated missing-person warrants, we based our care of the system's most high-risk and traumatised adolescents. It will come as no surprise that many of these adolescents enter adult forensic systems upon coming of age, and that their offspring often become part of the child protection system themselves. I have watched a number of familiar names from my time in child protection start trickling into the adult forensic system, with some dismay.

I stuck out my work in the lead tenant placement for several months in the hope that things would resolve, but moved out somewhat precipitously after starting to suffer some serious mental health impacts. I had most of the classic symptoms of PTSD for a few months (and looking back, would have met the criteria for a diagnosis); I was hypervigilant and startled whenever I heard a door slam (reminiscent of the front door at the property, and the danger signalled by someone unknown entering the house); I had frequent dreams of violence, sudden panics where I jumped thinking I heard screaming (it had been common for me to be woken by loud screaming from the room next door), my mood was disturbed, I was tired and irritable, and found it hard to settle enough to sleep. Luckily, I moved into a safe but busy house with some friends, and in that safety and bustle — as well as some sessions with my psychologist — I was able to shake my reaction before it took hold. Interestingly, I managed to work in the field of residential care work for a lot longer, perhaps because the harms and assaults I experienced there from clients were buffered by having a safe place to come home to.

The early indications of occupational trauma can be ambiguous. Less compassion than usual, more fatigue, some tiredness or bitterness, anger about having to go to work, stronger emotions than usual, mood swings, difficulties sleeping, increased alcohol use, withdrawal, a certain emotional deadness — these are the common signs reported to me. People often find it difficult to put the pieces of the puzzle together — many of these clues creep up unnoticed. We all have different signs; I know that irritability, resentment, and bad sleep/dreams are my main signals that things are awry. Education and reflection can be helpful, so that people know what symptoms to look for and can be aware of changes from their usual baseline, and understand and accept that occupational trauma can happen to anyone — it is not a personal failing.

Setting up systems that take occupational trauma seriously is essential. This means, in practice, that people are structurally supported to manage its effects, including easy access to appropriate treatment, paid time off to attend therapy, changes in duties as needed, reduced work hours, avoidance of stigmatisation and discrimination based on post-traumatic reactions, and support to maintain good mental health habits, including adequate rest and time between difficult clients. Screening to ensure that those with a diagnosis of PTSD receive targeted treatment is important, with other interventions for those who may be suffering from workplace stress and exhaustion. As always, prevention is better than cure; if we can accept that the nature of the work some people do is difficult and may lead to post-traumatic reactions, we can start to bring this knowledge into our workload planning, and the initial education and orientation provided to people. The alternative is that people burn out and leave, and the churn continues. Some professions, such as child protection services, have tacitly accepted this, but I am certain that this churn does nothing but perpetuate trauma for clients and professionals alike.

I referred to trauma-informed care earlier — this is an essential piece of the puzzle, not only for the victims we support, but also for professionals and colleagues who are exposed to trauma as part of their work. Trauma-informed care principles involve understanding the symptoms and how victims behave, supporting people to be fully involved in their physical and mental health care plans, holding their experiences in mind, and allowing them choices, agency, and mental and bodily autonomy. Realistically, this should be no less than any health service does for anyone, including its staff, regardless of a trauma history — but these basic principles of dignity, care, and compassion are overlooked or forgotten at times. Enshrining them within 'trauma-informed care' provides a framework to remind people of the vulnerabilities of people who seek healthcare.

Working within this framework means that we would be careful when establishing a person's circumstances (we usually do so by seeking collateral information where possible in forensic services, instead of retraumatising people by making them discuss all the difficult circumstances of their lives). We'd provide psychoeducation to clients, carers, and staff about what trauma responses can look like (e.g., sudden freezing may be a dissociative response to a perceived threat, not antagonism or non-compliance). We'd allow people agency and choice (such as by asking clients who are traumatised, but also aggressive, whether they'd prefer a time-out in a low-stimulus room or if they want some medication to help them settle). We'd use non-invasive mechanisms of management as much as possible regardless of setting (X-ray machines instead of strip searches in custody — though I note that Victorian prisons refuse to accept this valid alternative). We'd provide people with information about their diagnoses and offer them choices about treatment; we'd create safe and pleasant physical environments; we'd ensure that interventions such as seclusion are used as a last resort (and are certainly not used to manage suicidality), and we'd adopt attitudes of compassion, humility, responsiveness, and caring. Trauma-informed care also involves being perpetrator informed, with careful boundaries and limits on powers, oversight, mechanisms of complaint, and accountability for all, including all staff members holding power over vulnerable people.

None of this means that we are going to be pushovers — there are still times when we will have to set limits, say no, and assertively manage difficult situations — but we are likely to find that these times of crisis reduce when people feel safe, heard, and understood. Very traumatised people simply cannot respond to other people's hurt with sensitivity and clarity. Good trauma-informed systems of support involve deep regard for staff wellbeing — and can be revolutionary in reducing occupational trauma and staff burnout.

Conclusion

Why 'reclaim', you ask?

Reclamation is defined as the process of claiming something back or reasserting a right. It implies recapturing; dredging solid ground from the slow sulk of swamp, drifting tendrils of green over landscape charred by fires and devastation. It implies life, hope, growth — and the slow march of the new over what was once ruined. Reclamation is an apt metaphor when we consider the process of recovery from relational trauma, which so often involves a tediously slow process of meaning-making and sifting through; looking at devastated parts of a psyche and deciding which parts we can reclaim as solid ground and which parts we must let lie still. It suggests owning one's story fully, even the murky parts; it suggests speaking of the harms done to us and those things we have seen and overcome. To reclaim, we must survey, notice, and understand the damage, before slowly starting the work of dredging. We must go the long way sometimes, hold fast despite the tedium, until we can look at the new ground we have uncovered and say — *this is mine, I found this, I remade this.*

In this book, we have explored together the vast and difficult landscape of trauma reclamation. We have looked at the nature of complex trauma and the tasks needed for healing; examined the reasons that perpetrators behave in the manner they do; considered ways to manage those who might harm us; and ducked through the twisted alleys of the forensic system as we think about those victims who remain unseen. It has been a long journey, and you might be feeling fatigued or overwhelmed. Trauma and harm can be difficult subjects to think about. It can sometimes feel hopeless or too large.

The systems stacked against victims can feel overpowering. While it feels hopeless, though, there is much hope. We've made great strides in our knowledge about traumas, and in improving the ways we treat one another.

However, there is much work to do.

This book was conceptualised shortly after Grace Tame burst onto the public scene, and at a time when other alleged sexual assaults were being widely discussed. I was doing sexual assault–related trauma work with several clients at that time, and we often paused to talk about the rage they felt as they absorbed public commentary and saw that these harms continue to happen to so many women. They spoke of the ways in which their friends and family communicated that they didn't believe the women coming forward with allegations, said that Grace Tame was 'too angry' and thus unlikeable, and said that anyone who didn't tell other people right after an assault was probably lying. Many of my clients have never spoken of their histories to anyone except me, and they sat unseen during these conversations, shrinking into themselves.

I wrote this book for a few reasons, but primarily because unknowingly, we have created a world that is beset by trauma and allows many harms to continue, with very poor understanding of why people harm others, or the impacts on those who are harmed. We are shy and scared about speaking honestly about these harms, perhaps because we don't want to be eviscerated by the media or those who disagree, or don't want to shake up organisations and political systems, or maybe because it's simply easier to stay silent. I firmly believe that unless we approach this world with clear seeing, truth telling, and sincerity — we will never change it.

There is an appetite for change, that is clear, and in Australia we are moving toward increasing intolerance of some forms of violence, like sexual violence and intimate partner violence. However, we will never be able to change the incidence of interpersonal violence unless we open our eyes to the genesis of these behaviours, and can find systemic and individual ways to create change. This involves acknowledgement that we have got many things wrong and a genuine desire to do better, as we work on building a trauma-informed community.

This will look like many things.

Systemically, we will need to acknowledge that the social determinants of health (housing, income support, access to education, healthcare, and mental healthcare) are vital. We currently treat these factors as footnotes, bringing an individualistic lens to our interventions. Until we focus on building an equitable society where everyone can get their basic needs met, various forms of abuse and trauma will continue, and will cycle through generations.

We need to reduce our reliance on policing and incarceration-based responses. While I am a pragmatist and acknowledge that we need policing and incarceration (at least in our current society), these responses alone are not going to halt trajectories of harm. We also need forensically informed intervention services, geared toward truly understanding behaviours using multi-systemic research-driven models, and working closely on behaviour change while also supporting people to achieve positive life goals, like finding social connection and work.

We need to stop screaming for a tough on crime approach (this has been tested over decades, and it simply doesn't work). We need to stop building new prisons and funnel that money elsewhere. We need to raise the age. We need so much more funding for mental health services, especially for survivors of complex trauma. We need much better resourced and more trauma-informed child protection systems. We need to change the way in which we treat trauma victims in our adversarial court system. We need to explore restorative justice measures. We need juvenile justice systems that are therapeutic and focused on safety, sensible risk management, early multi-systemic intervention, and containment — *not* punishment. We need support for new parents, especially those considered at-risk. We need to stop burning out emergency and first responders, social services and healthcare staff — so they can keep doing the work they are committed to. We need to demand much more of the media as they talk about offending, violence, and harm. We need to demand zero tolerance policies for bullying at work. We need to do what we can to reduce occupational violence, and support those who are harmed at work.

Individually, we can also do much to be trauma informed.

First, and most importantly, we can reflect on our own behaviours, learn to be safe people, and learn to acknowledge and make reparations when we make mistakes. We can be harm-informed and keep an eye on those around us. We can be brave and speak up when we see injustices, even if it brings us censure. We can acknowledge that many unseen victims walk in our midst, and that we need to be sensitive with how we speak about trauma and harm. We can watch our levels of entitlement. We can stop closing our eyes to the difficulties around us to protect ourselves from feeling distress, and can instead learn to tolerate some discomfort in the pursuit of greater safety for all. We can teach the young people in our care about boundaries, respectful relationships, communication, emotions, and pleasurable and consensual sex. We can practise these concepts ourselves. We can learn to communicate anger calmly, without vitriol. We can demand action from our politicians.

As the world continues to veer toward geopolitical and climate crisis, we will need to be more firmly dedicated than ever before to staying the course, caring for ourselves and each other, and turning toward the harm we see. I realise that these tasks are a big ask, but if each of us exerts a small amount of influence and brings about change to the realms we inhabit, we can truly start to change the world.

For those who have read this book out of interest, I hope that you have a better understanding both of trauma and of those who abuse, and feel better equipped to notice, understand, and address wrongs as they arise, without resorting to the neat binaries and simplistic explanations often provided, and without needing to see people who harm as monsters. Far better to be realistic about those who harm, as that allows us to see and understand the harms caused by those who are not monsters. I hope you can be brave and strong and stand up for causes that matter.

For those with a trauma history reading these words — and for those who care for someone with such a history — I wish for kindness and gentleness, understanding, the ability to accept your stories, to reclaim and rewrite the parts of your being which have broken, to find safety in whichever way fits best for you and to know resilience and hope, without needing to find perfection. There is none, even in healing — there is just the gentleness of being enough.

Acknowledgements

These acknowledgements are a deeply felt thank-you for the contributions people have made to my work and this book, and for the broader care invested in me.

First, I must thank my excellent publisher and editor, Marika Webb-Pullman, for apologetically and politely sliding into my Instagram DMs (true story; it made up for all the unsolicited dick pics I have ever received) to ask if I wanted to write a book, for sharing my vision for *Reclaim*, providing painstaking and collaborative editorial guidance, and for holding such strong ethics in publishing. I love every minute of working with you.

Getting a book into the world requires the unstinting support of many people. Thank you to Cora Roberts, Guy Ivison, Mick Pilkington, Jessy Reese, Bella Li, Chris Grierson, Sarina Gale, Christopher Black, Marina Sano, and Josh Croggon at Scribe for all their support with bringing this book to life.

Thanks to Jack Smyth for the wonderful cover: gender neutral, triumphant, and hopeful!

Thank you to Emma Field, for the excellent advice about pitching, and to Stephane Shepherd, for the advice and encouragement to keep writing for the media, despite the initial deafening silence to my overtures.

I would like to thank Ingrid Ohlsson, for her support with formulating the first version of this work, and the encouragement to keep going with my manuscript.

Reclaim

Thanks also to the Wheeler Centre and Readings Foundation, for the support provided through the 2022 Hot Desk Fellowship Program.

Professionally, I must give thanks to numerous people within the broader ambits of psychology and forensic mental health. I truly do stand on the shoulders of giants.

Jim Ogloff, Michael Daffern, and Troy McEwan — you have all been hugely influential supports at pivotal points in my journey and have also been excellent role models of how to do this difficult work with clear thinking and compassion.

Merrilyn Hooley — your scaffolding of me during my initial psychology journey gave me the confidence to know I could go the distance. A very deeply felt thank you.

I must thank my wonderful team at the Problem Behaviour Program. I have learnt so much from all of you. You are some of the most compassionate, skilled, and incisive clinicians I know, and carry such risk and difficult work, with courage, care, and kindness for clients, and each other.

A big thank you to the wonderful psychologists who have supervised me over the years and supported me in this difficult work: Gregg Shrinkfield, Chris Drake, Jon Finch, Rachel Avery, and Simon Vincenzi.

Thank you to several other people at Forensicare, for supporting my work and writing in a range of ways, both operationally and clinically — Margaret Grigg, Anthea Lemphers, Aleksandra Belofastov, Lauren Ducat, Rachel Campbell, Melanie Starr, Kim Parker, and Anna Quinn. Thanks also to Abi Sheed, Israa Altwaijiri, Maddison Riachi, Madeleine Brygel, Annabel Chan, and Julia Nazarewicz for directing me to resources as I explored some thorny academic questions.

Personally, I have many people to thank.

To my family — I appreciate greatly the unconditional support and care you give me, and the joy you take in my successes. I am so

238

Acknowledgements

grateful for the encouragement to write and the support to pursue my dreams and live my somewhat non-linear life. Snigdha — sister, and amazing friend. I am truly lucky.

Kim, you have helped me transform my psychological makeup and thus, my life. This book is a testament to your work.

My wonderful friends — friendship is truly the ballast of my life, and I am so deeply grateful for all who inhabit my life: Steph with a Ph(D) Mathews (the best notBestFriendTM anyone could want), Anne and Alister Pate (and Daisy), Renee Middlemost, Martz Barkmeyer, Courtney Hammond, Amanda Nielsen, Shahera Souiedan, Jess Wilson, Brooke Underwood, Nikki Harrison (and Lenny longlegs), Kara Timion, Catherine Lander, Peter Bladin, Kalli Vakras, Adam Schroeder, Leanne Watson, Olivia Fitzgerald, Abi Sheed, Robyn Brown, Sarah Hartree, Will Sweet, Elise Whalan, Sarah Ambrose, Kia Sculthorpe, Poppy Edwards, and Emily Stevenson. There are others I may no longer be in touch with, but I nevertheless value the role you have played in my life.

Finally, Karla — being your ma is truly the very very very x1000 best thing my life holds. Everything is better with a snooty, snoozy, and disgruntled greyhound by my side. Luff you biggest, sweet potato.

Endnotes

A Note

1   Duffy, M. (2010). Writing about clients: Developing composite case material and its rationale. *Counseling and Values*, 54(2), 135–153.

Introduction

1   Kaler, S. R., & Freeman, B. J. (1994). Analysis of environmental deprivation: Cognitive and social development in Romanian orphans. *Journal of Child Psychology and Psychiatry*, 35(4), 769–781.

2   Guha, A., Luebbers, S., Papalia, N., & Ogloff, J. R. (2019). A follow-up study of mental health service utilisation in a cohort of 2433 sexually abused Australian children utilising five years of medical data. *Child Abuse & Neglect*, 90, 174–184.

     Guha, A., Luebbers, S., Papalia, N., & Ogloff, J. R. (2020). Long-term healthcare utilisation following child sex abuse: A follow-up study utilising five years of medical data. *Child Abuse & Neglect*, 106, 104538.

     Guha, A., Papalia, N. L., Luebbers, S., & Ogloff, J. R. (2020). Morbidity and mortality: Health outcomes and premature death in adult victims of child sex abuse. In *Child Sexual Abuse* (pp. 241–265). Academic Press.

3   O'Connor, S. S., Dinsio, K., Wang, J., Russo, J., Rivara, F. P., Love, J., ... & Zatzick, D. F. (2014). Correlates of suicidal ideation in physically injured trauma survivors. *Suicide and Life-Threatening Behavior*, 44(5), 473–485.

     Martin, M. S., Dykxhoorn, J., Afifi, T. O., & Colman, I. (2016). Child abuse and the prevalence of suicide attempts among those reporting suicide ideation. *Social Psychiatry and Psychiatric Epidemiology*, 51(11), 1477–1484.

4   https://www.forensicare.vic.gov.au/our-services/community-forensic-mental-health-services/problem-behaviour-program/

5   Warburton, K. D., & Scott, C. L. (2014). Violence risk assessment and treatment. *CNS Spectrums*, 19(5), 366–367.

6   Zimbardo, P. (2011). *The Lucifer effect: How good people turn evil*. Random House.

7   Dr Bessel A. van der Kolk, Dr Pat Ogden, Dr Peter Levine, and Dr Ellert R. S. Nijenhuis are some of the forerunners in this field.

2: The Impacts of Complex Trauma and Betrayal

1   Young, J. E., Klosko, J. S., & Weishaar, M. E. (2003). *Schema therapy:a practitioner's guide*. (New York: Guilford).

2   Thanks, David.

3   Schelling, G. (2002). Effects of stress hormones on traumatic memory formation and the development of posttraumatic stress disorder in critically ill patients. *Neurobiology of Learning and Memory*, 78(3), 596–609.

4   Porter, S., Yuille, J. C., & Lehman, D. R. (1999). The nature of real, implanted, and fabricated memories for emotional childhood events: Implications for the recovered memory debate. *Law and Human Behavior*, 23(5), 517–537.

5   Störkel, L. M., Karabatsiakis, A., Hepp, J., Kolassa, I. T., Schmahl, C., & Niedtfeld, I. (2021). Salivary beta-endorphin in nonsuicidal self-injury: an ambulatory assessment study. *Neuropsychopharmacology*, 46(7), 1357–1363.

6   Zerubavel, N., & Wright, M. O. D. (2012). The dilemma of the wounded healer. *Psychotherapy*, 49(4), 482.

7   Black, P. N., Jeffreys, D., & Hartley, E. K. (1993). Personal history of psychosocial trauma in the early life of social work and business students. *Journal of Social Work Education*, 29(2), 171–180.

8   Taylor, S. E., Klein, L. C., Lewis, B. P., Gruenewald, T. L., Gurung, R. A., & Updegraff, J. A. (2000). Biobehavioral responses to stress in females: tend-and-befriend, not fight-or-flight. *Psychological Review*, 107(3), 411.

9   Raemen, L., Luyckx, K., Palmeroni, N., Verschueren, M., Gandhi, A., Grobler, A., & Claes, L. (2021). Trauma and self-harming behaviors in high school students: The mediating role of identity formation. *Journal of Adolescence*, 92, 20–29.

3: The Trauma Survivor in the World

1   Van der Kolk, B. A. (2003). The neurobiology of childhood trauma and abuse. *Child and Adolescent Psychiatric Clinics*, 12(2), 293–317.

2   Thanks, Alister.

3   Perry, B. D. (2001). Bonding and attachment in maltreated children. *The Child Trauma Center*, 3, 1–17.

4   Levy, K. N., Blatt, S. J., & Shaver, P. R. (1998). Attachment styles and parental representations. *Journal of Personality and Social Psychology*, 74(2), 407.

5: The Difficult Trauma Victim

1   Ombudsman, V. (2019). OPCAT in Victoria: A thematic investigation of practices related to solitary confinement of children and young people.

2   Cauffman, E. (2008). Understanding the female offender. *The Future of Children*, 18(2), 119–142.

6: Why People Harm

1   Coid, J., Yang, M., Ullrich, S., Roberts, A., & Hare, R. D. (2009). Prevalence and correlates of psychopathic traits in the household population of Great Britain. *International Journal of Law and Psychiatry*, 32(2), 65–73.

2   Mitra P, Fluyau D. Narcissistic Personality Disorder. [Updated 2021 May 18]. In: StatPearls [Internet]. Treasure Island (FL): StatPearls Publishing;

2021 Jan-. Available from: https://www.ncbi.nlm.nih.gov/books/NBK556001/

3   McEwan, T. E., MacKenzie, R. D., & McCarthy, J. (2013). The Problem Behaviour Program: Threat assessment and management in a community forensic mental health context. *International handbook of threat assessment*, 360–374.

4   Fava, G. A., & Sonino, N. (2007). The biopsychosocial model thirty years later. *Psychotherapy and Psychosomatics*, 77(1), 1.

5   Tetlock, P. E. (1985). Accountability: A social check on the fundamental attribution error. *Social Psychology Quarterly*, 227-236.

6   Kuzelova, H., Ptacek, R., & Macek, M. (2010). The serotonin transporter gene (5-HTT) variant and psychiatric disorders: review of current literature. *Neuroendocrinology Letters*, 31(1), 4-10.

7   Day, A., Vlais, R., Chung, D., & Green, D. (2018). Standards of practice in domestic and family violence behaviour change programs in Australia and New Zealand. *Australian and New Zealand Journal of Family Therapy*, 39(4), 501–513.

8   Herman, K., Rotunda, R., Williamson, G., & Vodanovich, S. (2014). Outcomes from a Duluth model batterer intervention program at completion and long term follow-up. *Journal of Offender Rehabilitation*, 53(1), 1–18.
     Snead, A. L., Bennett, V. E., & Babcock, J. C. (2018). Treatments that work for intimate partner violence: Beyond the Duluth Model. In *New Frontiers in Offender Treatment* (pp. 269–285). Springer, Cham.
     Dutton, D. G., & Corvo, K. (2006). Transforming a flawed policy: A call to revive psychology and science in domestic violence research and practice. *Aggression and Violent Behavior*, 11(5), 457–483.

9   Napier, S., Dowling, C., Morgan, A., & Talbot, D. (2018). What impact do public sex offender registries have on community safety?. *Trends and Issues in Crime and Criminal Justice*, 550, 1–20

10   Yim, I. S., & Kofman, Y. B. (2019). The psychobiology of stress and intimate partner violence. *Psychoneuroendocrinology*, 105, 9–24.

7: Identifying Harmful People

1   Australian Bureau of Statistics. (2021). Sexual Violence – Victimisation. Report, Canberra, ACT.

2   Australian Institute of Health and Welfare. (2018). Family, domestic and sexual violence in Australia 2018. Cat. no. FDV 2. Canberra: AIHW.

3   Bryant W & Bricknell S. (2017). Homicide in Australia 2012–13 to 2013–14: National Homicide Monitoring Program Report. Canberra: AIC.

4   https://www.anrows.org.au/media-releases/young-australians-confused-about-consent-and-control-in-the-age-of-tinder-and-snapchat/

5   Galletly, C. A. (2004). Crossing professional boundaries in medicine: the slippery slope to patient sexual exploitation. *Medical Journal of Australia*, 181(7), 380–383.

6   https://www.abs.gov.au/media-centre/media-releases/36-million-people-experienced-partner-emotional-abuse

9: The Politics of Trauma

1   Dutton, D. G., & Corvo, K. (2007). The Duluth model: A data-impervious paradigm and a failed strategy. *Aggression and Violent Behavior*, 12(6), 658–667.

2   McEwan, T. E., Shea, D. E., Nazarewicz, J., & Senkans, S. (2017). Reassessing the link between stalking and intimate partner abuse. *Partner Abuse*, 8(3), 223–250.

3   Drijber, B. C., Reijnders, U. J., & Ceelen, M. (2013). Male victims of domestic violence. *Journal of Family Violence*, 28(2), 173–178.

4   Badour, C. L., Blonigen, D. M., Boden, M. T., Feldner, M. T., & Bonn-Miller, M. O. (2012). A longitudinal test of the bi-directional relations between avoidance coping and PTSD severity during and after PTSD treatment. *Behaviour Research and Therapy*, 50(10), 610–616.

5   Johnson, M. P. (1995). Patriarchal terrorism and common couple violence: Two forms of violence against women. *Journal of Marriage and the Family*, 283–294.

6   http://rcfv.archive.royalcommission.vic.gov.au/MediaLibraries/
    RCFamilyViolence/Statements/WIT-0064-001-0001-Ogloff-9_1.pdf

7   Testa, M., Hoffman, J. H., & Leonard, K. E. (2011). Female intimate partner
    violence perpetration: Stability and predictors of mutual and nonmutual
    aggression across the first year of college. *Aggressive Behavior*, 37(4), 362–373.
    Graham-Kevan, N., & Archer, J. (2009). Control tactics and partner violence
    in heterosexual relationships. *Evolution and Human Behavior*, 30(6), 445–
    452.
    Daff, E. S., McEwan, T. E., & Luebbers, S. (2021). Australian adolescents'
    experiences of aggression and abuse by intimate partners. *Journal of
    Interpersonal Violence*, 36(9–10), NP5586–NP5609.

8   Langhinrichsen-Rohling, J. (2010). Controversies involving gender and
    intimate partner violence in the United States. Sex Roles, 62(3), 179–193.

9   Boxall, H., Doherty, L., Lawler, S., Franks, C., & Bricknell, S. (2022). The
    "Pathways to intimate partner homicide" project: Key stages and events in
    male-perpetrated intimate partner homicide in Australia (Research report,
    04/2022). ANROWS.

10 Australia's National Research Organisation for Women's Safety. (2022).
    Pathways to intimate partner homicide: The "fixated threat" offender
    trajectory [Fact sheet]. ANROWS.

11 The AIC study describes this typology of offender: 'FT offenders constituted
    one third of all IPH offenders in the study (33%, n=59). Despite being jealous,
    controlling and abusive in their relationships, FT offenders were relatively
    functional in other domains of their life. In many cases they were typically
    middle-class men who were well respected in their communities and had
    low levels of contact with the criminal justice system. Their abusive behaviour
    often took the form of controlling, stalking and monitoring behaviours
    which escalated in the context of the victim's perceived withdrawal from
    the relationship (e.g. separation). Among FT offenders, IPH was used as
    a means to re-establish control over the victim or in other domains of his
    life that he blamed her for his loss of control over (e.g. his access to their
    children).' See reference '9' for more information.

12   Bonta, J., & Andrews, D. A. (2007). Risk-need-responsivity model for offender assessment and rehabilitation. *Rehabilitation*, 6(1), 1–22.

13   Cermak, P., & Molidor, C. (1996). Male victims of child sexual abuse. *Child and Adolescent Social Work Journal*, 13(5), 385–400.

14   Carmo, R., Grams, A., & Magalhães, T. (2011). Men as victims of intimate partner violence. *Journal of Forensic and Legal Medicine*, 18(8), 355–359.

15   Herrenkohl, T. I., & Jung, H. (2016). Effects of child abuse, adolescent violence, peer approval and pro-violence attitudes on intimate partner violence in adulthood. *Criminal Behaviour and Mental Health*, 26(4), 304–314.

16   Hamby, S., Finkelhor, D., Turner, H., & Ormrod, R. (2016). Children's Exposure to Intimate Partner Violence and Other Family Violence (2011).

17   Diamond, A. (2002). Normal development of prefrontal cortex from birth to young adulthood: Cognitive functions, anatomy, and biochemistry. In D. Stuss & R. Knight (Eds.)*Principles of frontal lobe function*, (466–503). New York: Oxford University Press.

18   Wolfe, D. A., Wekerle, C., Scott, K., Straatman, A. L., & Grasley, C. (2004). Predicting abuse in adolescent dating relationships over 1 year: the role of child maltreatment and trauma. *Journal of Abnormal Psychology*, 113(3), 406.

19   Sindicich, N., Mills, K. L., Barrett, E. L., Indig, D., Sunjic, S., Sannibale, C., ... & Najavits, L. M. (2014). Offenders as victims: post-traumatic stress disorder and substance use disorder among male prisoners. *The Journal of Forensic Psychiatry & Psychology*, 25(1), 44–60.

20   Ball, R., & Walters, A. (2017). Total control: ending the routine strip searching of women in Victoria's prisons. Human Rights Law Centre.

21   Ombudsman, V. (2019). OPCAT in Victoria: A thematic investigation of practices related to solitary confinement of children and young people.

10: Caring for the Carer

1   Walker, A., McKune, A., Ferguson, S., Pyne, D. B., & Rattray, B. (2016). Chronic occupational exposures can influence the rate of PTSD and depressive disorders in first responders and military personnel. *Extreme Physiology & Medicine*, 5(1), 1–12.